ADVENTURE TIME CRAFTS

ADVENTURE TIME CRAFTS

FLIPPIN' ADORABLE STUFF TO MAKE FROM THE LAND OF OOO

CARTOON NETWORK.

PRINCESS BONNIBEL BUBBLEGUM
WITH CHELSEA BLOXSOM

PHOTOGRAPHY BY TAMARA STAPLES

POTTER
CRAFT

NEW YORK

Published in the United States by Potter Craft, an imprint of the Crown
Publishing Group, a division of Random House LLC, a Penguin Random House
Company, New York.
www.crownpublishing.com
www.pottercraft.com

POTTER CRAFT and colophon is a registered trademark of Random House LLC.

ADVENTURE TIME, CARTOON NETWORK, the logos, and all related characters
and elements are trademarks of and © Cartoon Network.
(S14)

Library of Congress Cataloging-in-Publication Data
Bonnibel Bubblegum, Princess of the Candy Kingdom.
  Adventure time crafts : flippin' adorable stuff to make from the Land of Ooo /
by Princess Bonnibel Bubblegum with Chelsea Bloxsom and Cartoon Network.
— First edition.
1. Handicraft. I. Bloxsom, Chelsea. II. Cartoon Network (Television network) III.
Adventure time (Television program) IV. Title.
  TT157.B685 2014
  745.5—dc23   2013045906

ISBN: 978-0-8041-8566-0
eBook ISBN: 978-0-8041-8567-7

Printed in China

Design by Stephanie Huntwork
Photography by Tamara Staples
Illustrations by Phil McAndrew
Illustrations on pages 29 and 131 by Kevin Stanton
Photos on pages 57–59 by Sarah Waite
Illustration on page 109 by Chantal Lavender

10 9 8 7 6 5 4 3 2 1

First Edition

Welcome to my crafty kingdom, dear do-it-yourselfers! This little book of projects and inspiration is your guide to the adventure of making cute stuff with your own two hands.

I am such a huge nerd for creating stuff, whether it's concocting candy people in my laboratory or knitting a sweater for a friend. Handmade things make mad special presents! Nothing says "I like you a lot" quite like a gift you took the time to make yourself.

The citizens of Ooo (and the outer reaches of Lumpy Space) have inspired thousands of fans to stitch, sculpt, paint, and otherwise craft delightful works of handmade art. This book brings together a dazzling array of handmade fashion, charming toys for kids and grown-ups of all ages, decor to deck out your digs, and other ideas that will add candy-colored fun to your world.

You shall also be pleasantly surprised to find that many of these projects don't require special tools or extraordinary skills. If you can thread a needle, you're good to go. (And if you can't . . . well, there's always fabric glue!) More advanced projects are also included, as I hope they will inspire you to pick up a fun new hobby.

So let's start flexing those creative muscles and limber up for a major craftathon. It's gonna be bloobaloobie! —PRINCESS BONNIBEL BUBBLEGUM

CHAPTER 1

It's freaking adorable.

TOTAL TOYTOPIA

I firmly believe that no one is ever too old to play with toys. If you enjoy watching cartoons, then you are still a child at heart!

Small toys are perfect for trying out new craft techniques and getting comfortable with the tools and materials you will need to use for more complicated projects later in this book. Break out the pointy needles, hot-glue guns, and stacks on stacks of felt. Peeps'll never be bored in my crafty empire!

Reenact your favorite episode of *Adventure Time™*, or invent one entirely your own with these finger puppets and stage. You choose which parallel universe you want to live in: Finn and Jake's or Fionna and Cake's!

The puppets and stage utilize a lot of supplies that you might already have around the house. Assembled with a little hand stitching and fabric glue, the puppets whip up fast for maximum cuteness. If you're making the stage with little kids, make sure that a responsible adult is in charge of the craft knife.

YOU WILL NEED

Fan Fiction Finger Puppets templates (page 129)

Felt in colors corresponding to each character

- Finn: white, cream, pink, blue, light green, green
- Fionna: white, cream, yellow, blue, light green, green
- Jake: yellow-orange, white, black
- Cake: white, tan, black
- Princess Bubblegum: pink, yellow-orange, cream, purple, dark pink, blue
- Prince Gumball: pink, yellow-orange, purple, cream, hot pink, blue
- Marceline: black, gray, dark gray
- Marshall Lee: gray, black, red

Scissors

Sewing needle

Sewing thread to match felt

Embroidery thread in black and red

Fabric glue

Cardboard box

Ruler

Pencil

Acrylic or poster paints

Paintbrush

Craft knife

Hot-glue gun

Cotton fabric

Sewing machine (totes optional!)

Two buttons

Lumpy Space Princess Pom-Pom Mobile templates (page 130)

Marker

Card stock

FAN FICTION FINGER PUPPETS STEPS

1   Using the templates (page 129), cut out pieces of felt in colors corresponding to each character following the list of materials (A).

2   With matching thread and blanket stitch (page 124), sew the main body pieces together for each character. Leave the bottom of each puppet open for your finger.

   NOTE: When sewing Cake and Prince Gumball, make sure to sandwich Cake's ears and Gumball's crown in between the body pieces with a running stitch (page 127).

A

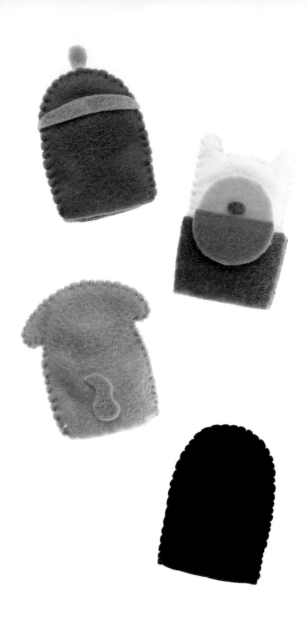

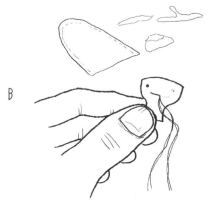

B

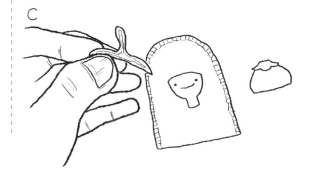

3 Embroider the facial expressions onto the face pieces before adding each face to the body. For Finn, Fionna, Bubblegum, Gumball, Marceline, and Marshall Lee, use French knots (page 126) to stitch their eyes with black embroidery thread (B).

4 Add details as indicated in the templates, with a back stitch (page 124): Embroider two red dots each on Marceline's and Marshall Lee's necks for their vampire bites. Embroider a line down Marshall Lee's shirt in black, and the plaid lines in gray. Embroider a little line on Prince Gumball's neckpiece.

5 Using fabric glue, attach each face and other details to the main body. Spread a thin layer of glue on the back of the face or detail, wait a few minutes, then add another layer (C). Press the piece into the body piece. Let dry completely before using.

C

ADVENTURE TIP

These small puppets are a great way to use up leftover scraps of felt from other projects. Sort small pieces of felt by color into clear zip-top bags, and you'll have a fabric stash to dip into when you need just a little bit of one color.

FAN FICTION STAGE STEPS

1 Find a cardboard box (a pancake batter mix box works perfectly) and turn it inside out. Using a ruler to create straight lines, mark a rectangle ¾" (2cm) from the sides of the piece that will be the front of the stage. Mark out a trapezoid shape, approximately 2" (5cm) tall on the side of the box that will be the bottom (D).

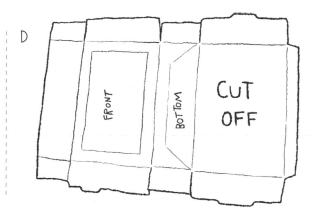

D

FRONT

BOTTOM

CUT OFF

2   Use a craft knife to cut out the shapes you have created on the box. Paint the outside of the box in a solid color. Let dry. Place a heavy book on the cardboard to prevent it from warping. With a hot-glue gun, glue the flaps of the box together. Hold each section until it dries.

3   Cut out two rectangles of cotton fabric for the curtains. Each curtain should be 1½" (3.8cm) taller than the back of the stage and equal the length of the stage so they will cover the entire back.

4   Flip the two pieces of fabric over, fold the top of the fabric ¾" (2cm) down, and pin in place. With a sewing machine (or by hand), stitch a straight line ¼" (6mm) from the folded edge to make a pocket.

5   Thread a long length of embroidery floss through a needle and knot one end. Insert needle through the side edge of the stage, and then thread one of the buttons onto the floss, on the outside of the side edge. Pull the needle until the knot hits the side of the box. Sew an X into the button, and then bring the needle and thread to the inside of the stage again. Thread the needle and floss through the curtains and poke through the other side of the stage to sew the second button in place (E). Hot-glue the ends of the curtains to the edge of the stage.

E

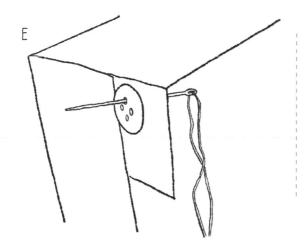

6 Using the small star template from Lumpy Space Princess Pom-Pom Mobile (page 130), cut out four stars. Glue one star to each corner of the stage.

Cut out a half-oval shape and write "Land of Ooo" on top of it. Using decorative scissors or by hand, cut it into a starburst shape. Glue onto the top of the stage.

NEEDLE-FELTED GUNTER

The Ice King's head henchman (henchpenguin?) is the most evil creature you'll ever encounter. He can only quack, but you can see the lust for evil in his cold, cold eyes. These miniature guys are deceptively cute decorations for your desk, dashboard, or even tied to the top of a gift package.

In this project we'll learn needle felting, a beginner-friendly craft, using sharp, precise needles to shape little balls of wool into rounded shapes. Be very careful when doing this craft because the needle is extremely sharp and this tutorial works with some very small pieces.

YOU WILL NEED

Wool roving in black, white, and yellow

Felting needle

Foam felting pad

NOTES:

• This toy has small parts and is not suitable for kids under age 3.

• Felting needles are serious business, dude. Be careful you don't stab your fingers!

STEPS

1 Take the black roving and separate it into five pieces for Gunter: one large piece for the body shape, two medium-sized pieces for the wings, and two small pieces for the eyes. Leave a little extra roving to help smooth out the shape at the end of the project instructions.

2 Roll the large piece into an egg shape. Secure the ends of the wool by jabbing the felting needle into them. Felting needles have a serrated edge that helps the wool stick to itself. Start to shape the body piece by jabbing evenly across it. Don't stab it too much in one place or it won't be smooth. Shape the bottom so it's flat and the piece can stand up. The wool should be felted just enough so that it's spongy when you squeeze it.

A

3 Once you're happy with the body shape, take a piece of the white roving and fold it over. It should be just slightly smaller in height than the body shape. Lay the piece on the felting pad and start to jab it into the general shape of Gunter's belly (A).

4 Place the belly piece on top of the body piece. Begin to jab into the belly, starting at the edges first so the belly secures itself to the body, and then evenly throughout so the fibers adhere. Be careful not to pull any of the black fibers over the white or it will look messy.

Wenk! Wenk!

ADVENTURE TIP
If you're looking for an unusual craft material, like felting needles and wool roving, check out my shopping guide (page 122) for a list of retailers I recommend.

5 When the stomach is smoothed out, take a tiny piece of the yellow roving and twist and fold it into the shape of Gunter's beak. Make sure it's pretty thin, as his beak is skinny. Carefully jab the beak, holding it between your fingers to shape it, while leaving the part that will attach to the body fairly untouched.

Attach the beak, jabbing around the perimeter of the beak base with short jabs and then longer jabs farther up. Give it a gentle tug to make sure the wool is fused.

6 For the eyes, roll each of the two small pieces of black wool roving into a ball. Pull each piece tight and check it against the body to make sure it's the amount you want. Carefully poke it between your fingers, turning it as you go to make a nice, even circle.

Before it gets too stiff, adhere each black circle to the body right above the beak, using long jabs into the body piece. Pull each circle gently to make sure it's stuck to the body.

7 Take two pinches of white roving for the pupils. One at a time, hold each piece between your fingers and jab at it gently while turning it to make a tiny pancake shape. Adhere each white circle to the middle of a black circle by poking around the perimeter of the white (B).

8 Take two even lengths of black roving and fold one of them into itself to form a basic wing shape. Place it on the needle-felting pad. Jab each wing to seal, and then turn and jab at it evenly to shape. Leave the end unworked.

Place the wing on the body piece where you want it to be attached, and stab at the unworked area until the wing adheres to the body. Shape and attach a second wing with the other piece of black roving.

B

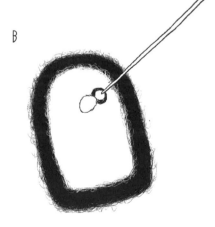

Hmm. You're looking kinda fat, Gunter! Look at these arms! Fat, fat, fat! Daddy's little fattie! Oh, you'll never get a prom date with all that chub on your face, you know!

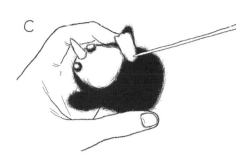

C

9   Take two small pieces
    of yellow roving and fold
    each into a penguin foot
    shape. Stab at the wool to
    mold it, making extra stabs
    between the toes. Leave
    the part that will attach to
    the body unworked.

        Attach the feet to the
    body piece through the
    unworked part. Jab at the
    wool until the foot stays
    in place, pulling gently to
    make sure it's adhered (C).

10 If parts of your penguin
    look dented or uneven,
    you can take a small piece
    of roving and add it to the
    finished toy, gently jabbing
    until the shape is smooth
    and rounded.

Whoa!
Felt-O-Rama!

Any character with simple, rounded shapes
would make a great needle-felted toy, using the
same technique you just learned in this project.
Here are a few ideas to get you started:

- Hot Dog Princess is an elongated
  oval, with four nubs for feet in slightly
  lighter brown. Try using small beads
  for her eyes and nose, and cut out
  yellow paper to make an adorable
  crown!

- Tree Trunks has an almost perfectly
  round body, in chartreuse green. To
  make her limbs and trunk, needle-felt
  the wool around a short length of cord.
  Don't forget to tie a pink bow around
  her tail!

- BMO is a bit of a challenge, with lots
  of details in different colors. After
  shaping the rounded boxlike body,
  create the small colorful buttons on a
  felting pad before applying them to the
  front of the character.

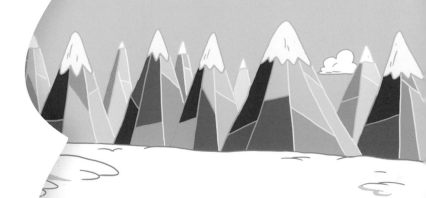

LUMPY SPACE PRINCESS POM-POM MOBILE

There are no age limits when it comes to crafty stuff, and this sassy mobile would look just as beautiful hanging in your science lab as it would over a baby's crib. As it gently spins, you can almost hear Lumpy Space Princess's singing voice lulling you to sleep.

You'll learn some sweet tricks to use in other crafts, such as making 3D stars and the easiest, peasiest way ever to make pom-poms out of yarn. Once you get into this project, you won't be able to stop making pom-poms (or stop talking like LSP!).

YOU WILL NEED

Lumpy Space Princess Pom-Pom Mobile template (page 130)

10" (25.5cm) embroidery hoop

Yarn in white, purple, and yellow

Scissors

White embroidery floss

Embroidery and sewing needles

Felt in black, yellow, and pink

Card stock in yellow

White sewing thread

Hot-glue gun

I know you want to slump up on these lumps, But you can't 'cause you're a ch-uuuump.

A

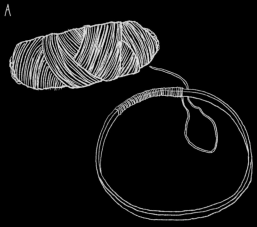

STEPS

1 Attach the white yarn to the inner circle of the embroidery hoop (the piece without the clasp), securing the yarn with a knot. Slowly wrap yarn around the hoop, covering it completely, and secure the other end with a knot. Tuck the end of the yarn underneath some of the yarn wrapped around the hoop (A).

2 Thread a long length of the white embroidery floss onto a needle and thread through a few pieces of yarn on the inside of the hoop. Tie a knot at the very end so it stays in place. Loop the floss over a few times to secure it. Bring the thread to the exact opposite side of the hoop, leaving a lot of slack in the middle. This length of slack floss will determine how far the mobile will hang. Knot the thread on the inside of the hoop as you did on the first side.

3 Take another length of the white floss and cross over the first thread perpendicularly. Make sure it's the same length as the first. Hold the thread where it crosses in the middle to make sure it hangs evenly, and then tie the two threads together in a loop on the top.

4 Make a bunch of pom-poms! You'll need 20 in total: 5 white, 10 purple, and 5 yellow. (See Makin' Pom-Poms, page 25.)

5 Assemble Lumpy Space Princess with 6 purple pom-poms. Make sure the pom-poms (or "lumps") are all as uniform as possible. Starting with the top lump, hot-glue all 6 pom-poms together into a triangle formation (B) and hold the pieces together briefly to let cool. Be careful the glue doesn't soak through to the other side, and press pieces of yarn over any visible glue marks.

B

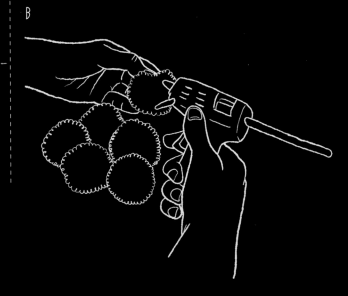

6   Cut out the pattern pieces for LSP's face following the templates (page 130). Create two sets of felt pieces, one for each side. Use the hot-glue gun to secure all the face pieces, pressing lightly. Trim up the edges of the pom-pom to make her look nice 'n' lumpy.

7   Cut out all the star pieces using the templates (page 130). Three pieces are used for each 3D star. There are 7 small 3D stars in total on this mobile, and 1 large 3D star. For each 3D star, fold two of the pieces in half.

8   Make two small 3D stars as follows: Cut a length of embroidery floss about 7" (18cm) and thread onto the needle. With the hot-glue gun, make a line of hot glue through the middle of the star. Quickly press the end of the embroidery thread into the glue, followed by the crease of one of the folded stars. Flip the star over and run a line of hot glue down the middle, and then press the other folded star into the glue.

C

9   Thread the white embroidery floss with the star on it through the right bottom lump (C). Stitch it back and forth a few times to secure, and trim the excess. Repeat for the left bottom lump.

10 Take an extralong length of the embroidery thread and knot one end. Thread the other end on a needle, and starting at the bottom center lump, pull the thread through the top lump of LSP. Tie the floss through the loop on the top of the mobile. Leave enough room so LSP is hanging just below the embroidery hoop.

11 Following the instructions in Step 3, attach one large 3D star onto a piece of embroidery floss. Attach one small 3D star to the floss above the first star, leaving about the height of one small star between them. Attach the floss to the middle lump.

Oh, my Glob! What the stuff are you doing?! Why are you cutting my lumps?!

12 Using 6" (15cm) strands of sewing thread (not embroidery floss), make four more small 3D stars. Attach each of the four remaining 3D stars to the bottom of the embroidery hoop equidistant from each other by knotting the thread between pieces of yarn on the hoop. Let them hang about 2" (5cm) from the hoop.

13 Arrange the remaining pom-poms in two sets of three in a row, and two sets of four in a row following the photo.

Knot the end of a piece of sewing thread, and thread the other end onto a long sewing needle. Thread the needle through the middle of the bottom pom-pom, and then the other two in the order they will hang.

14 Sew the lines of pom-poms in between the stars, arranging the set of three and set of four directly across from each other on the hoop. Move the pom-poms up and down on the thread to balance the mobile.

Makin' Pom-Pom Steps

1 Wrap yarn around your fingers, using two fingers for the smaller pom-poms and three for the larger. To make varying sizes use the thicker part of fingers for some, and fingertips for others.

2 Keep wrapping until there is a thick amount of yarn around your fingers. The more yarn, the thicker the pom-pom will be.

3 Carefully slide the yarn off your fingers, and tie a piece of the yarn around the center of the entire ball of yarn, pulling tight. Flip it over and double-knot on the other side.

4 Cut the loops on either side. Pull the yarn pieces up and trim the pom-pom. It look scraggly at first, but the more you trim it, the nicer it will look.

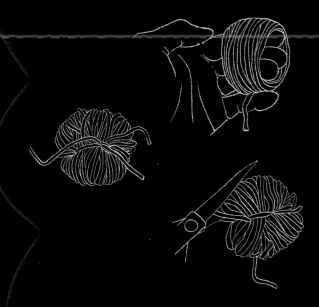

MARCELINE'S AXE BY THE SILVERED BLADE

J am out as Marceline and make your own axe worthy of the Vampire Queen herself. This fun prop lets you play some mean air bass as you sing some of her songs, or complete a totally accurate Marceline costume. When you get back from the convention, it would look flippin' awesome hanging up on your wall.

This project involves a lot of spray paint and craft knives, so take your time and make sure you have a well-ventilated space. If you have access and skills to use basic woodworking tools, you can choose to make this project with wood instead of cardboard.

YOU WILL NEED

Marceline's Axe templates (page 131)

Sheet of cardboard, at least 24" x 36" (61cm x 91cm)

Card stock in white or ivory

Scrap newspaper

Spray paint in red and silver

Repositionable glue stick

Craft knife and extra blades

Self-healing cutting mat

Craft paint in dark red, silver, and black

Flat, soft paintbrush

Wood glue

Daddy, why did you eat my fries? I bought them, and they were mine.

La da da da da,

I'm gonna bury you in the ground,

La da da da da,

I'm gonna bury you with my sound . . .

STEPS

1 Trace the templates (page 131) and prep the cardboard. Lay out some scrap newspaper (an artist's tarp or old sheet works well too) in a well-ventilated outdoor area. Spray the cardboard with at least two coats, minimum, of the red paint to make sure the color is nice and opaque. Three coats might work better to fill in any gaps in the paint. Spray the card stock with the silver paint (twice or thrice, again).

2 Mount the pattern marked "body" to the back (unpainted) side of the cardboard with the repositionable glue stick. Mount the pattern marked "details" to the back (unpainted) side of the card stock with the glue stick.

3 Place the cardboard, painted side down, on the cutting mat. Using the craft knife, carefully cut into the cardboard following the printed black lines. For optimal results, cut a light outline that penetrates the first layer of the cardboard. Then slowly cut a bit deeper for a second pass, which should cut through the corrugated part of the cardboard. Finally, you should be able to carefully cut a final outline to release your pieces from the main pieces of cardboard. This is the step that takes the most time, but being careful with cardboard is worth the effort, as you don't want it to rip. If it does, though, you can always cut a new piece!

4 Place the card stock silver side down on the mat. Card stock is much easier to cut than cardboard, but go slowly on the curves to keep it as clean as possible. Carefully peel off the printer paper from the backs of your pieces.

ADVENTURE TIP
When you are enlarging patterns from a smaller template, it's often worth the extra cost to take it to your local print shop. Make sure to let them know that it is a large-format print and needs to be printed on a plot that is 24" x 36" (61cm x 91cm).

5 Paint the details. On the top layer of the neck, paint a black X on the head, and thick black lines down the neck. I painted thirteen lines, seven near the base of the guitar that are close together, and then six evenly spaced lines that end at the bottom of the head (the topmost line shown).

6 On the middle layer of the body, use the dark red to paint a wide margin. The middle part of this layer doesn't show, so there's no need for a clean line. Then paint the little triangle at the bottom with silver craft paint. This step may need two coats, as silver craft paint is rather transparent. On the head layer shaped like a pentagon, paint the "tuning pins" silver. This layer doesn't show except for the pins, so again there's no need for clean lines.

7 Glue the cardboard layers as shown in the illustration with wood glue (A). When the guitar is put together and dry, carefully glue the silver detail pieces also using the wood glue. If you want, you can flip it over and spray the red, but I like the unfinished cardboard look, personally.

A

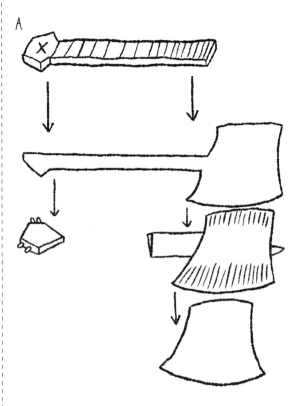

REVERSIBLE JAKE/CAKE PLUSH

Everyone could use a sidekick like Cake or Jake to go on adventures with, but how can you choose between the two? Now you don't have to. Make this reversible Jake and Cake plush and you can switch sides for whatever story you're in!

A sewing machine is definitely helpful for this project, but not necessary. If you choose to sew the toy by hand, use a back stitch (page 124) when adhering the body pieces together. This will create a stronger seam so the plush can withstand years of flying, shape-shifting, and troublemaking.

YOU WILL NEED

Reversible Jake/Cake Plush templates (page 132)

Fleece in white and yellow-orange

Felt in white, black, and pink

Scissors

Sewing needles and thread

Sewing machine (optional, but helpful)

Polyester fiberfill

Pencil or other pointed tool

NOTE: If you don't want to make a reversible toy, check out the pattern modification (page 35) to make a single character.

Catnip! Sweet babies!

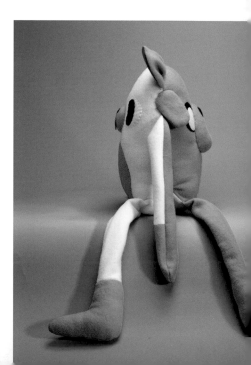

ADVENTURE TIP
Whenever you are instructed to turn a piece inside out, use a pointed tool to push out all the nooks and crannies. This will ensure that the seams are nice and neat on the outside of the toy. You can use a specialty point turner, or just wing it with something conveniently on hand. A spare pencil, chopstick, or candy cane all work great!

STEPS

1   Scale the Jake/Cake Reversible Plush templates (page 132) to the size you want the toys. I enlarged the reversible toy to 300 percent and the individual Jake and Cake toys to 150 percent.

2   Cut out the pattern pieces. For the reversible option, do not cut out the tails or back pieces, and only cut one side of each character's arm. Cut out the main body, ears, and limbs in fleece. Cut out the eyes, noses, tongue, and the inside of Cake's ears in felt (A).

3   Pin the feet onto the bottom of the leg pieces for Cake, and pin her different-colored arm pieces together. Run through the machine or hand-stitch using a back stitch (page 124) to secure.

A

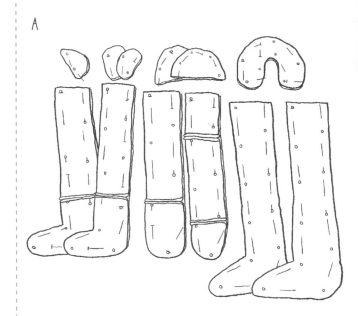

4   Pin the arms, legs, ears, and Jake's muzzle with right sides together. Pin one side of Jake's arm to one side of Cake's arm. Run them all through the machine, leaving an opening at the ends to turn them right side out.

5   Pin Cake's stomach and eye spots onto the body piece, and then sew in place by hand or with a machine. Pin Cake's eyes down and sew. Then sew the pupils on top of the eyes.

6   Sew the darts on Cake's muzzle together. Turn around and hand-sew the nose on top, and embroider a small mouth and a line down the tongue so it still sticks out (B).

    Pin the muzzle between the eyes, and sew around the edge until there's a small hole. Push stuffing into it with the back end of a pen or a pointed tool. Close up the hole.

B

7 Slightly fold Cake's ears in the middle between your hand. Pin each ear to her head. Flip it over and mark either side with a pen.

8 Take the Jake side and pin down the black parts of the eyes. Sew them down and then appliqué the white portion on top.

9 Pin the legs down on both Jake and Cake, flip over and mark either side. Unpin the ears and legs and set them aside.

10 Take the arms and figure out where you want them to hang from on the body. Pin them into place, with them folded in toward the body so it looks like it's hugging itself. Tuck the ends of the arms in so they don't get in the way (C).

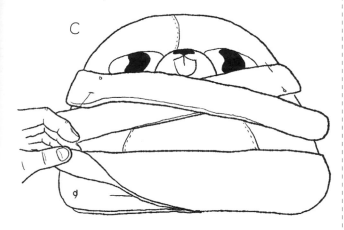

C

11 Take the bottom piece and pin half of it to the bottom front side of Cake. Place the Jake piece on top facing Cake, and pin the other half of the bottom to his bottom. Pin the rest of the body together. Run through the sewing machine, or hand-sew, omitting the gaps you marked for the ears and legs.

12 Unpin and turn right side out through one of Cake's earholes. Unpin the arms and put your hand through one of the holes to smooth out the seams. (Use a pen if your fingers can't reach.)

13 Stuff the legs, pushing the polyester fiberfill down with a pen into the end of the feet up to the ankle. Put the stuffed legs into the hole gaps, yellow-orange on the Jake side, white on the Cake side. Pin into place and sew into the body using a back stitch (page 124).

14 Stuff the toy through the earholes. If you want added weight on the bottom, you can use fabric scraps (D).

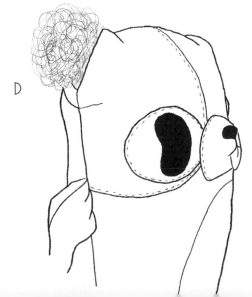

D

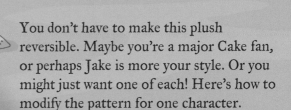

15 Pin the ears back into the earholes once it's all stuffed. Sew into the body using a back stitch.

16 Stuff Jake's muzzle and close the hole using a ladder stitch (page 126). Use a running stitch (page 127) to sew the nose onto the top of the muzzle.

Lightly stuff Jake's ears and close the holes using a ladder stitch. Stitch Jake's ears and muzzle onto the body.

ADVENTURE TIP

You'll notice that three different types of stitches are recommended for this project. Instructions for each technique are included in Crafty Basics (page 124), but if you have trouble mastering a particular stitch, there are also many homemade videos on YouTube. Fellow crafters are very generous about sharing their knowledge, so don't be shy if you need extra help!

I'm gonna go rescue all the babies in town. Only the babies.

You don't have to make this plush reversible. Maybe you're a major Cake fan, or perhaps Jake is more your style. Or you might just want one of each! Here's how to modify the pattern for one character.

- When cutting out the pattern pieces, make sure to cut one back piece for the character in fleece, including Cake's spot. Also cut out two tails from fleece.

- Follow the instructions in the reversible pattern *only* for the character you are interested in making. When it comes time to pin the Jake and Cake sides together (Step 11, page 34), use the back piece in place of the opposite character. Continue project instructions as written.

- Pin the two sides of the tail, with right sides facing, and sew around the perimeter, leaving the top open. Turn and stuff. Attach the tail to the back of the toy using a ladder stitch.

CHAPTER 2

BLING-A-DING-DING

Designing your own jewelry is so very satisfying. Whenever you get a compliment on something you crafted yourself, you can proudly claim, "Actually, I made it!"

This chapter is full of fancy little things to wear. I love these projects because I can mix and match them for any occasion: a Lady Rainicorn ring when I'm chilling with my bestie, a BMO ring to accessorize a more casual outfit, or pretty hair adornments for formal royal events. These projects make great gifts for all your friends. And sparkly crafts are always a hit at slumber parties, too!

CANDY KINGDOM FRIENDSHIP BRACELET

This painted bracelet has the power to imbue the wearer with great knowledge of science, morality, and the ability to flirt with cute boys. I designed it as a reminder that gumdrops, cinnamon rolls, lollipops, and other sugary treats can all live together in harmony.

In this project, we'll sculpt, bake, and paint polymer clay beads to resemble the diverse community of my hometown, the Candy Kingdom. It will get you comfortable working with polymer clay, so you can build up to more advanced projects later in the chapter. Of course, you can add as many more sweet citizens as you'd like for a longer bracelet or even a necklace!

YOU WILL NEED

Polymer clay in various colors (red, white, green, blue, yellow, brown, purple—whatever colors you want!)

Acrylic paint in various colors (I used black, white, yellow, blue, green, pink, red, and brown)

Toothpicks or skewers

Detail paintbrush

Parchment paper

Kitchen oven or toaster oven (see notes)

Elastic cord

Scissors

Needle

Cardboard

Pins

Clear acrylic glaze

NOTES:

- Parchment paper is available at most grocery stores, often next to the waxed paper. It's a great investment for your craft cabinet, because you'll use it in many other projects that involve baking or ironing.

- Never bake polymer clay directly on the surface of a baking sheet that you use for food.

- If you are concerned about releasing polymer fumes in your kitchen oven, place the piece inside an aluminum foil oven bag. Many polymer clay artists use a dedicated toaster oven just for curing their clay.

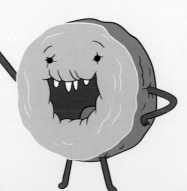

In the Land of Ooo is a Candy Kingdom whose sidewalks you can eat.
And everyone who lives in there is made of something sweet.

ADVENTURE TIP
I invented some new Candy Kingdom characters just for this project, and I encourage you to do the same! Just give them tiny beady eyes, goofy expressions, and pastel or bright, neon colors and they will fit right in!

STEPS

1 Roll out a small amount of polymer clay between your palms to create a ball. Make one large ball, ¾" (2cm), in pink for Princess Bubblegum, and then make smaller balls, until you have enough to go around your wrist—I ended up with 12 smaller beads total for this bracelet.

2 With a toothpick, gently press into the middle of the balls with a twisting motion. When the ball is all the way on the toothpick, reshape the clay to make it look nice again. Skewer two beads on each toothpick (A).

A

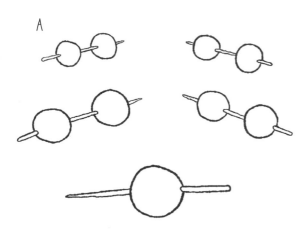

3 Place a piece of parchment paper on a baking sheet, and then lay the full toothpicks on the parchment paper. Bake according to the temperature and time indicated by the polymer clay manufacturer. (Different brands of polymer clay have different requirements.)

4 When the beads are done, immediately put them in a cup of ice water. Leave them there for a few minutes, and then put them on a paper towel to dry; this will help the colors' vibrancy.

5 Now it's time to paint! If you want larger details like hot fudge drips or whipped cream hair, paint them first with the detail brush and wait for the paint to dry (B).

NOTE: Holding the beads on toothpicks makes it easier to work with them.

B

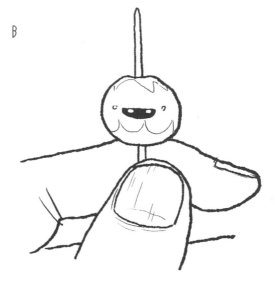

6 Use the pointy end of a toothpick dipped in paint to create mouth lines and teeth, and make circles with the blunt end of the brush for sprinkles or for eyes.

7 After you've added all the details you want, paint two thin, even layers of clear acrylic glaze on each bead.

8 To prevent the beads from moving around, stick a sewing pin through the top of each bead into a thick piece of cardboard. Let the beads dry. Rearrange the pinned beads on the cardboard until they are in the order you want for the finished bracelet (C).

C

9 Double a long length of elastic, and knot the ends. Make the knot thick enough that the first bead won't fall off the elastic.

10 Thread the folded end of the elastic through the eye of a needle, and then thread the beads in the order you decided on. Next, pull the needle through the two pieces of knotted elastic on the other end, and pull fairly tight so all the beads touch each other. Then double-knot the ends together, and snip off the excess. Tuck the knot in between two beads.

ADVENTURE TIP
To turn this project into a pair of earrings, follow the instructions in the Best Buds Mismatched Earrings (page 52) to add jewelry findings.

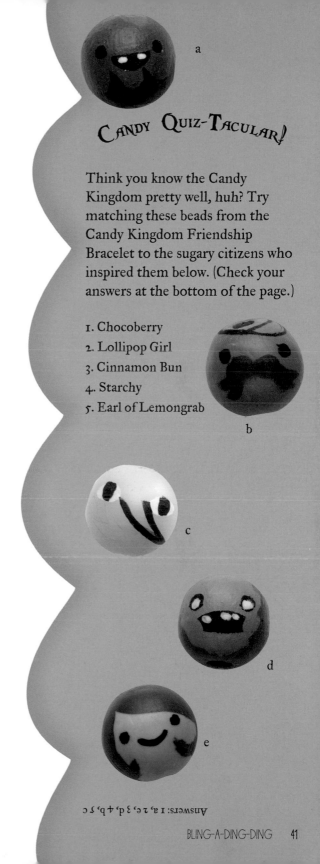

CANDY QUIZ-TACULAR!

Think you know the Candy Kingdom pretty well, huh? Try matching these beads from the Candy Kingdom Friendship Bracelet to the sugary citizens who inspired them below. (Check your answers at the bottom of the page.)

1. Chocoberry
2. Lollipop Girl
3. Cinnamon Bun
4. Starchy
5. Earl of Lemongrab

a

b

c

d

e

Answers: 1 a, 2 e, 3 d, 4 b, 5 c

SHRINK-A-COW-TASTIC EARRINGS

Shrinky Dinks® are one of the coolest crafts ever. If you draw on these plastic sheets and bake them in an ordinary kitchen oven, they will shrink into hard plastic charms. Try not to squeal with excitement as you watch your hand-drawn designs suddenly transform in the oven. (I couldn't help it.)

This is a great craft to do if you only have a little bit of time to make something! The craziest thing about it? You can make a butt-ton of projects all using the same basic technique. You'll learn the ropes with these sweet earrings featuring Finn's sword, but turn the page for even more project ideas.

YOU WILL NEED

Shrink-a-Cow-Tastic Jewelry templates (page 135)

Shrink plastic (a.k.a. Shrinky Dinks®)

Black permanent marker

Colored pencils

Scissors

Hole punch

Cookie sheet

Parchment paper

Baby powder

Kitchen oven or toaster oven

Book

Brush-on sealant (Mod Podge®)

EARRINGS ONLY
Dangling earring backs

Jump rings

LADY RAINICORN RING ONLY
Wooden dowel or marker
(see notes)

NOTES

- Cookie sheets, parchment paper, and baby powder are all available at the grocery store.

- If you're making another type of project (page 45), you may need a key-chain ring or necklace chain and clasp.

SWORD EARRINGS STEPS

1   Place the shrink plastic over the template for the design you want (page 135) and outline the shapes with permanent marker on the smooth side of the plastic. Keep in mind that the designs will shrink down to a little over one-third of the size once they're baked in the oven. For earrings, repeat this step to prepare another charm.

2   Flip the plastic over to the frosted side and fill in the designs with colored pencils. Only color over the black marker with black colored pencils, and don't press down too hard. The colors will get much more vibrant as the plastic shrinks and the colors move closer together. For details like the scratches on the hilt of Finn's sword, use a metallic silver colored pencil that can color over the darker colors.

3   Carefully cut the design out from the shrink plastic (A). With the hole punch, create a hole where you'd like the charm to hang from an earring back, or other jewelry finding.

A

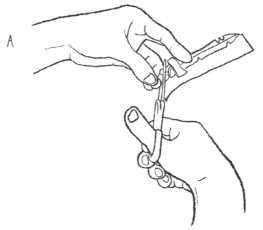

4   Prep the earrings and your kitchen oven. Place a sheet of parchment paper to cover the cookie sheet and sprinkle a tiny bit of baby powder on top of the parchment paper; this will keep the designs from sticking to themselves or the paper. Preheat the oven to 350°F. Put the cookie sheet and parchment paper in the oven while it's preheating so the designs will bake more evenly and quickly.

5   Once it's preheated, place the designs on the parchment paper and close the door (B). They should shrink within a minute of being in the oven. Don't worry if it looks like they're warping and wiggling—they should straighten themselves out. If not, carefully use a toothpick to unstick the design from itself.

B

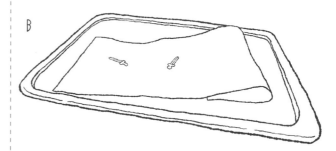

ADVENTURE TIP
The secret to shrink plastic is science, of course! This material is also known as recycled plastic #6, which is made up of tangled polymers. When the plastic is heated, the polymers straighten out and move closer together, shrinking the plastic to one-third of its original size.

6   When it looks like the plastic has stopped shrinking, pull the parchment paper out of the oven, and place a book on the charms briefly to keep them from warping. They'll harden and cool very quickly.

7 Brush each side lightly with the sealant to prevent scratches. Wait for it to dry.

8 Using a pair of pliers or your fingers, hook one jump ring into each hole. Attach another jump ring to the first, and then the earring backs (or other jewelry findings). This will create a nice dangle and make sure each charm faces the right direction. If you're making a Lady Rainicorn pendant, attach two jump rings to either side, and then to the necklace chain.

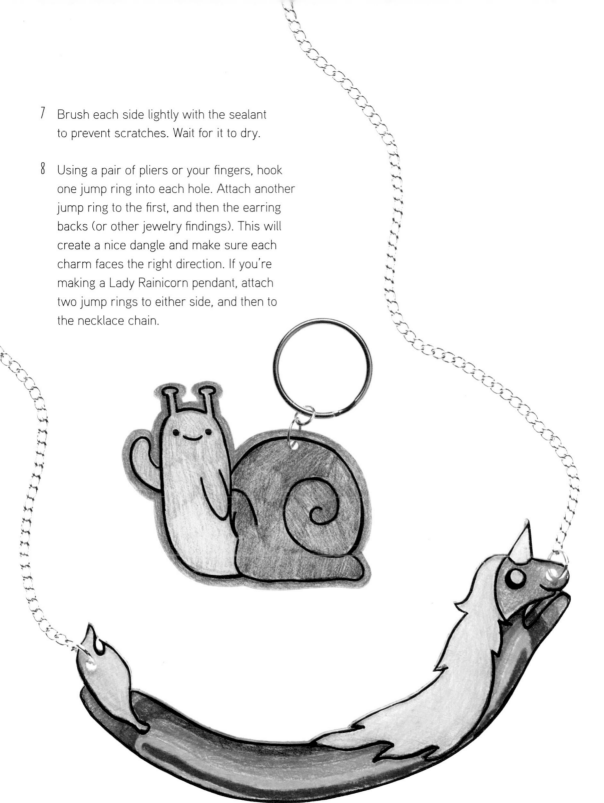

LADY RAINICORN RING STEPS

1 Shrinky Dinks® don't have to be simply flat shapes. To make a cool wraparound ring follow Steps 1–5 for one sword earring (pages 43–44), without punching a hole for jewelry findings. Bake the charm as normal.

2 When the shrunk plastic comes out of the oven, wait a second or two, and then carefully (but quickly!) wrap the plastic around a wooden dowel or marker that matches the circumference of your finger. Wrap the Lady Rainicorn charm in a spiraling motion up the dowel so that the ends do not overlap (C).

C

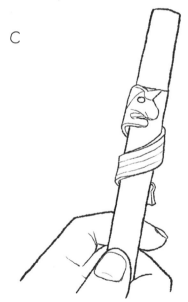

3 If it comes out warped the first time around, you can place the plastic back in the oven so it flattens back out, and try again.

More Shrink-A-Cow-Tastic Magic

Here are a few other projects to make with shrink plastic, complete with all the templates you need to trace them (page 135).

- Turn Marceline's Axe (bass guitar) into some totally mathematical earrings. Use a metallic silver pencil to draw in the strings, just as you did for the sword earrings. These look great with your favorite rock band T-shirt.

- If you like the sweet and cute side of the Candy Kingdom, color in a Lady Rainicorn pendant to sweep across your neck. Punch a hole on each end of the shrink plastic before you cure it in the oven.

- The Snail key chain is a supersneaky, supershrinky way to show your *Adventure Time*™ fandom. Punch one hole before you shrink the plastic, and later attach the jump ring to a key-chain ring.

- If you have a piece of fan art that you just love, print it out to three times the scale that you want your finished piece to be. Trace the art onto a piece of shrink plastic, and go for it! I recommend starting with simpler shapes (like my self-portrait earrings) and then building your artistic repertoire from there.

POLYMER POWER PENDANT AND RING

As with shrink plastic, polymer clay cures in an ordinary home kitchen oven. Use this colorful material to sculpt durable charms, and then add various different jewelry findings to make pendants and rings!

The best part about these projects is that you don't need a lot of material to make them. A small block of polymer clay lasts for a few projects. Save your scraps to use in the Best Buds Mismatched Earrings (page 52)! Polymer clay miniatures require a steady hand to create the tiny adorable details, so make sure to take your time with each piece.

YOU WILL NEED

Polymer clay in various colors

- Gunter: black, white, and yellow-orange
- BMO: teal and white

Toothpick or pointy clay tool

Craft knife

Parchment paper

Kitchen oven

Scissors or nail clippers

GUNTER PENDANT ONLY

26-gauge wire

Necklace chain

Two jump rings

Necklace clasp

Needle-nosed pliers

White or black acrylic paint (optional)

Clear acrylic glaze

BMO RING ONLY

Sandpaper

Blank ring back

Rubbing alcohol or nail polish remover

Acrylic paint in black, red, yellow, blue, white, and green

Instant adhesive glue

NOTES:

- Before sculpting with a new color of polymer, always wash your hands. Clean fingers will help you avoid smudging different colors of clay.

- Never bake polymer clay directly on the surface of a baking sheet that you use for food.

- Many polymer clay artists use a dedicated toaster oven just for curing their clay.

- If you are concerned about releasing polymer fumes in your kitchen oven, place the piece inside an aluminum foil oven bag.

PENDANT STEPS

1 Lay down a sheet of parchment paper on your work surface. Roll out a fat oval of black clay for Gunter's body. Tap the bottom of the clay on the parchment paper to make a flat bottom.

2 Cut a small square of black clay in half. Press each piece flat and sculpt into wing shapes. Press the wings onto either side of Gunter, and smooth down the top edges.

3 Wash your hands and then press out a piece of white clay very flat. Cut into the shape of Gunter's body piece. Hold up to the body to compare until it's the shape you want. Carefully press the white clay onto the black oval and slightly smooth the edges, making sure not to get any black clay onto the white (A).

4 Roll out a small egg of yellow-orange clay. Cut the egg in half and slightly press the pieces to create the feet.

   Press the feet onto the bottom of Gunter's body. Tap the whole piece on the parchment paper a few times to make sure the bottom is still flat. Make little toe indents using a toothpick.

5 Roll out a thin long cone for the nose and cut the end for a nice crisp edge. Carefully press the beak on top of the white belly, pinching to keep its nice shape.

6 Roll out two tiny balls of black clay, and two tiny balls of white clay. Press flat into nice circles, the white circles slightly smaller than the black. Press the black clay on either side of the beak, followed by the white on top.

A

7 Snip a piece of the wire about 1½" (3.8cm) long with the nail clippers or scissors. With pliers, twist one end into a loop. At the other end of the wire, make a loop and twist the wire a few times around it to secure it. Snip off the excess.

8 Using the toothpick, press a hole into the center top of Gunter's head. Push the wire down into his head until only the second loop you made is showing from the top. Lightly pinch the clay around it, or if necessary, smooth a little bit of clay around the hole to secure (B).

B

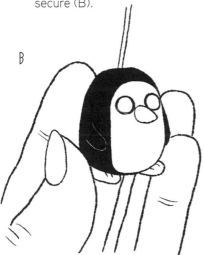

9 Place the Gunter pendant charm on a piece of parchment paper lining a baking sheet. Bake, following the polymer clay manufacturer's instructions.

10 Drop the charm into a cup of ice water immediately after taking it out of the oven and leave it in there for a few minutes. Pull it out and let dry.

11 When it's dry, you can paint over any dirty-looking parts of Gunter using black and white acrylic paint. Then paint over the entire piece with two thin even coats of clear acrylic glaze.

12 When the glaze has dried, place a jump ring through the wire loop. Thread the needle chain through the jump ring, and cut to your desired length. Using pliers, open the jump ring and clasp and attach to either end of the necklace.

ADVENTURE TIP
There are many different brands of polymer clay on the market, so try out a few to discover which one you like to work with best. Pay particular attention to the temperatures and suggested baking times on the package, as each formula of clay requires slightly different conditions to properly cure.

BMO RING STEPS

1 Pinch together a teal rectangle about 1"
(2.5cm) tall and a little over ½" (13mm) wide.
Press to about ⅛" (3mm) thick. Use a craft
knife to sharpen the edges.

2 Mix teal and white clay to make BMO's face
by rolling two thin ropes of each clay, twisting
them together, and then kneading the clay
until the colors are evenly combined. Press
a piece of the mixed clay down so it is thin
and flat. Cut a small rectangle with the craft
knife. Compare the face to the body until you
like the size, then press the light teal onto the
darker teal block (A).

3 Using the ring back, make an indentation
in the back of BMO where it's going to be
placed (B).

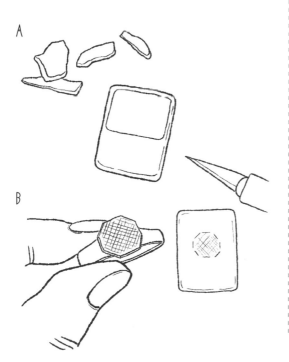

4 Bake BMO on a piece of parchment paper
on a baking sheet, following the polymer clay
manufacturer's recommended temperature
and time.

5 While it's baking, use sandpaper to sand off the
finish on the pad of the ring back. Clean the
pad with a cotton swab and rubbing alcohol to
help the charm adhere to the ring better.

6 When the charm is done, immediately drop
it in a cup of ice water. Leave it in for a few
minutes, then place on a paper towel.

7 Once dry, use a toothpick and acrylic paints to
carefully add the details, following the photo. If
you mess anything up, you can erase it with a
little bit of water on a piece of paper towel or
cotton swab before the paint dries.

8 When the paint is dry, add two thin, even
coats of clear acrylic glaze.

9 Dot just enough glue to cover the pad. Press
the pad into the indentation on the back of
BMO and hold. Scrape off any excess glue
with a toothpick. Wait 24 hours for the glue to
dry before wearing.

BEST BUDS MISMATCHED EARRINGS

Finn and Jake are like two peas in a pod. They've had some fights, but at the end of the day they can always set aside their different tastes in movies. Although these earrings are mismatched charms, they're still an inseparable pair.

Now that you've tried out a few polymer clay projects, it's time for a slightly more difficult challenge. Slow down while you're creating the small details in this project. If you mess up, you can always mush the scraps together to make painted beads for other projects, such as the Candy Kingdom Friendship Bracelet (page 38).

YOU WILL NEED

Polymer clay in white, yellow-orange, cream, and black

White acrylic paint

26-gauge wire

Toothpick or clay poker tool

Craft knife

Parchment paper

Needle-nosed pliers

Clear acrylic glaze

Four jump rings

Two dangling earring backs

Scissors or nail clipper

Kitchen oven

NOTES:

- Before sculpting with a new color of polymer, always wash your hands. Clean fingers will help you avoid smudging different colors of clay.

- Never bake polymer clay directly on the surface of a baking sheet that you use for food.

- If you are concerned about releasing polymer fumes in your kitchen oven, place the piece inside an aluminum foil oven bag.

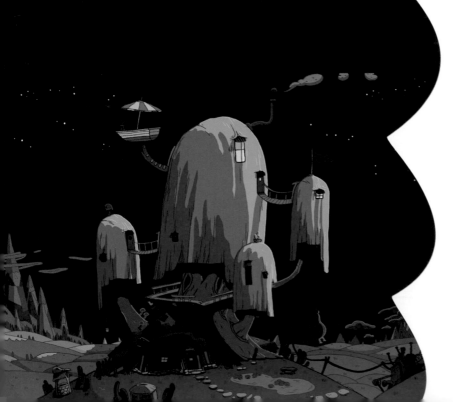

STEPS

1 Place a sheet of parchment paper on your work surface. Work the yellow-orange clay in your hands to make it pliable. Roll out an oval about 1" (2.5cm) long and press it slightly flat on each side on a piece of parchment paper for Jake's head.

2 With a toothpick or clay tool, indent the ears on either side of Jake.

3 Roll out two small thin tubes of the yellow-orange clay for Jake's muzzle. Bend them into U shapes and lightly press around to slightly flatten. Set aside.

4 Roll six very small balls of black clay. Take four and press flat using an edge of the parchment paper. Make them as even as possible. Push and smooth two onto either side of Jake's face using the toothpick or your fingers. Press the other two into small ovals for the noses (A).

A

5　Wash your hands of the black clay before handling the white clay. Take four slightly smaller balls of white clay and press into flat circles. Carefully place and push on top of the black circles.

6　Press the muzzle piece between the eyes, and then the little nose piece on top of it on both sides. Make nostrils with the pointy end of a toothpick.

7　Snip a piece of the wire about 1½" (3.8cm) long with the nail clippers or scissors. Use the pliers to twist one end into a loop (B).

Take the other end and make a loop and twist the wire a few times around it to secure it. Snip off the excess.

B

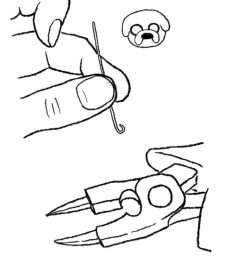

8　Using the toothpick, press a hole into the center top of Jake's head. Push the wire down into the charm until only the second loop you made is showing from the top. Lightly pinch the clay around it, or if you need to, smooth a little bit of clay around the hole to secure. Set the Jake charm aside.

9　Wash and dry your hands and roll out an oval of white clay the same size as the Jake charm, pressing it slightly flat.

Roll out a tiny oval of white clay, and then cut in half for Finn's hat ears. Carefully press the ears to the larger white oval and smooth out the edges.

10　Take two balls of the cream clay and press thin and flat. Use a craft knife to cut out the oval for Finn's face. Smooth out the edges and press onto each side of the white oval.

11　Roll four small balls of black clay for the eyes. Make indents in the face and press the eyes into them (C).

C

12 Flatten two small pieces of black clay, and cut out little half-ovals for Finn's mouth. Press each mouth between the eyes.

13 Following the instructions in Step 7, make another wire loop for the Finn charm.

14 Put the charms on a piece of parchment paper on a baking pan. Bake at the polymer clay manufacturer's recommended time and temperature.

15 Have a glass of water and ice ready for when the charms come out of the oven, and immediately drop them in. Leave them in the water for a few minutes, then take them out and place them on a paper towel. (This step is optional but will make your pieces more durable.)

16 Once they've dried, touch up Finn and Jake with the white acrylic paint in any areas where they may look "dirty" from smudging the clay with other colors. Paint Finn's teeth using white acrylic paint and a toothpick.

17 While Finn's drying, take the Jake charm, holding the wire loop between your fingers or a binder clip, and give him two thin, even coats of clear acrylic glaze. Then do the same to Finn.

18 When the glaze is dry, pull open the jump rings with a pair of pliers, and join the rings in this order: wire loop, jump ring, jump ring, and earring back. Make sure each wire loop is securely closed.

Oh, you a-a-a-a-are, my best friend in the world. You a-a-a-a-are my best friend in the world.

ADVENTURE TIP
These charms don't have to be earrings. Follow the instructions for making pendants and rings (page 48), and then try mixing up the characters and jewelry styles. Do you want to make matching BMO earrings? Finn and Jake necklaces? A whole handful of different rings? Go crazy!

OH MY GLOB, NAIL ART! BY CHALKBOARD NAILS

You'll be looking fresh to death with your new dress and purse once you accompany that outfit with these lumpin' awesome nails! Brad will totally want to get back together with you. This tutorial offers three different designs so you can mix and match your manicure however you'd like.

For a craft project, nail art is fairly quick and easy, but it takes some patience and a steady hand. If you're feeling proficient at painting details, give each finger a different LSP face for an even sassier style. With your fingers looking this good, you gotta put a ring on it, babe!

YOU WILL NEED

Toothpick or small nail art brush

Dull pencil or dotting tool

LSP purple nail polish (Illamasqua *Jo'mina*)

Yellow nail polish (China Glaze *Happy Go Lucky*)

Black nail polish (American Apparel *Hassid*)

Dark gray nail polish (LCN *Tokyo Expression*)

Purple glitter nail polish (Different Dimension *That Is So Fetch*)

Topcoat (Seche Vite Dry Fast Topcoat)

Oh, my Glob! Yes!

I'm gonna be so hot!

So freakin' hot!

LSP'S FACE STEPS

1 Paint your nails with two coats of purple polish and let dry. Dip a dull pencil or dotting tool into the black polish, and use it to dot two eyes about halfway down your nail.

2 Using a toothpick or nail art brush and black polish, paint on LSP's eyebrows. One of them should sit just above the eye, and the other should be slightly raised. Using the gray polish, apply an ellipse for the mouth just below the eyes. Be sure to set it slightly off center!

3 Outline the ellipse with black polish, and add a curved cheek off to the side.

4 Begin creating LSP's star by using the yellow polish to make a five-pointed guide.

5 Continue making the outline of the star by extending two lines out from the point of each guide line.

6 Finally, fill in the star with yellow. Let dry. Finish your manicure with topcoat for seal and shine.

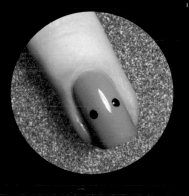

SINGLE STAR STEPS

1 Paint your nails with two coats of purple polish, let dry, then use a toothpick (or nail art brush) and the yellow polish to make a five-pointed guide.

2 Extend two lines out from the point of each guide line.

3 Fill in the outline you've made with yellow nail polish and let dry. Finish your manicure with topcoat for seal and shine.

GLITTER FADE STEPS

1 Paint your nails with two coats of purple polish. Let dry.

2 Load up as much of the purple glitter polish on the nail polish brush as you can. Pile the glitter polish near your cuticle.

3 Working quickly, wipe the nail polish brush off. Then go back and use the clean brush to drag some of the glitter down toward the tip of your nail. If needed, apply more glitter near the cuticle. Let dry.

NOTE: Use a light hand when dragging and don't go too far down the nail!

4 Finish with topcoat for seal and shine.

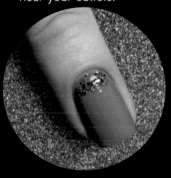

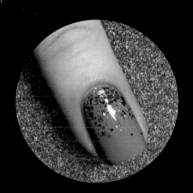

Whatever, just don't touch my beans.

There certainly are a lot of princesses in the Land of Ooo. There's a princess of fire, a princess of slime, a princess of breakfast, a princess with muscles, a princess of hot dogs— and yours truly, of course! So I designed these individual hair accessories in collaboration with a few of my fellow rulers.

In this project, you'll get to customize the ribbon, colors, size, and character that suits your personality and style, and choose between a bobby pin, barrette, or fascinator. You can even make the set of four and wear them all together! Just watch out for the Ice King. That guy turns into a real patoot when he sees a bunch of princesses.

YOU WILL NEED

Princess Hair Adornments templates (page 136)

Felt in various colors to match character

- Flame Princess: orange, yellow-orange, pink
- Lumpy Space Princess: purple, yellow-orange
- Slime Princess: lime green, beige, yellow
- Princess Bubblegum: pink, cream, yellow-orange, blue

Blank hair accessories: barrette (2¾" [7cm] long), bobby pin (2" [5cm] long)

Ribbon for bows, approximately 1–1½" (2.5cm–3.8cm) wide

Scissors

Pen

Hot-glue gun

Sewing needle

Sewing thread to match felt colors, plus black

NOTE: Your local pharmacy store or beauty supply shop will have lots of options for different clips and barrettes. Or try attaching your bow and appliquéd motifs to a plastic comb, as for the Wildberry Princess Fascinator (page 66).

FLAME PRINCESS HAIR BOW STEPS

1 Cut out three strips of ribbon: one ½" x 2¾"
   (13mm x 7cm, or big enough to cover the
   top of the barrette), one 1½" x 8" (3.8cm x
   20.5cm), and one ¾" x 3½" (2cm x 9cm).

2 Mark the middle of the longest strip with
   a pen. Put a small line of glue down the
   center and fold in the ends of the ribbon to
   the middle. (Don't overlap the ends.) Put a
   dot of glue in the center of the ribbon and
   pinch down. Bring the other two sides into
   the center like an accordion and glue them
   down (A).

A

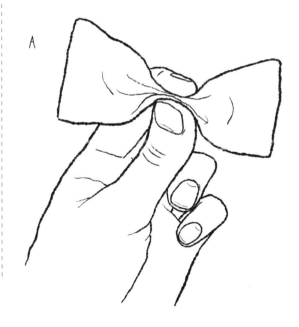

3 Hot-glue one end of the ¾" x 3½" (2cm x 9cm) piece of ribbon to the center back of the bow. Hot-glue the ½" x 2¾" (13mm x 7cm) piece of ribbon to the top of the barrette. Then glue the bow on top of the ribbon.

4 Wrap the ribbon twice around the middle of the bow, through the barrette, and down the back. Hot-glue in place and trim the excess (B).

B

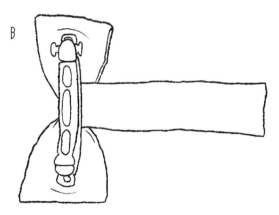

5 Using the template (page 136), cut out all the pattern pieces for the face appliqué from felt, making sure to cut two pieces of the head shape.

6 Appliqué Flame Princess's bangs onto one of the head pieces with matching thread. With black sewing thread, embroider the mouth and eyebrows using a back stitch (page 124), and make tiny French knots (page 126) for the eyes. If you get confused, just follow the stitch key next to the template.

C

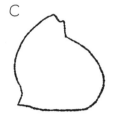

7 Place the second head shape behind the first one. Use a blanket stitch (page 124) and matching thread to neatly sew them together (C). Finally, hot-glue the face to the center of the bow.

ADVENTURE TIP

If you'd rather wear one of these hair adornments as a snazzy bow tie, knock yourself out! Instead of a barrette, secure the appliqué felt face and the bow to a wide ribbon long enough to comfortably fit around your neck. Secure the ends with a snap or Velcro.

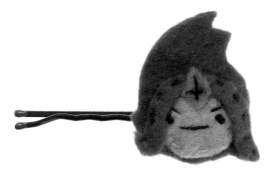

FLAME PRINCESS BOBBY PIN STEPS

1   Cut out all Flame Princess pieces from felt following the template (page 136). For a bobby pin, only cut out one main head piece. Appliqué the face onto the main head, and then appliqué the Flame Princess's bangs on top.

2   With embroidery floss, stitch the facial features. Use a back stitch (page 124) where the template indicates and create French knots (page 126) for the eyes.

3   Cut a small rectangle of orange felt and slip it between prongs of the bobby pin. Hot-glue the sides of the small felt rectangle onto the back of the head to secure the face in place.

You should not toy with the emotions of a fire elemental.

ADVENTURE TIP
Don't feel like sewing on the facial features? Just use a fine-tipped fabric pen or fabric paint with a small detail brush. Personally, I prefer embroidery, but there's nothing wrong with taking a shortcut here.

LUMPY SPACE PRINCESS HAIR BOW STEPS

1   This hair bow is actually created with two loops of ribbon, instead of one. Cut out four strips of polka-dot ribbon: one ½" x 2¾" (13mm x 7cm, or big enough to cover the top of the barrette), two 1" x 7" (2.5cm x 18cm), and one 1" x 4" (2.5cm x 10cm).

2   Take each of the 1" x 7" (2.5cm x 18cm) strands and fold them following the instructions in Step 2 of the Flame Princess Hair Bow (page 61). Then hold the two loops together to create a double bow and continue to the next step.

SLIME PRINCESS HAIR BOW STEPS

Use three pieces of green satin ribbon (for a slimy appearance) to replace the two strands of 1" x 7" (2.5cm x 18cm) ribbon used in the Lumpy Space Princess Hair Bow.

Greetings, loyal slimejects!

PRINCESS BUBBLEGUM HAIR BOW STEPS

1 To make the mega double bow used in the
   Princess Bubblegum barrette, use four
   pieces of thin ribbon ⅝" x 7½" (1.6cm x
   19cm) long, one ½" x 2¾" (13mm x 7cm),
   and one 1" x 4" (2.5cm x 10cm). Otherwise,
   the technique is exactly the same for creating
   the Flame Princess Hair Bow (page 61).

2 Take each of the long strands and fold
   them following the instructions in Step 2
   of the Flame Princess Hair Bow (page 61).
   Then hold the 4 loops together to create a
   quadruple bow and continue to the next step.

WILDBERRY PRINCESS FASCINATOR

Fascinators are extralarge hair adornments that look great with updos. If the other princess appliqués have too many fiddly little pieces for you, try practicing your stitches with this project first.

YOU WILL NEED

Wildberry Princess Fascinator template (page 136)

Felt in raspberry, green, light pink

Plastic comb (2¾" [7cm] wide)

Scissors

Hot-glue gun

Sewing needle

Sewing thread to match felt colors

Embroidery floss in black

STEPS

1 Cut out all the Wildberry Princess pieces from felt following the template (page 136). Appliqué the face to one of the head pieces with matching thread, and hot-glue the stem and leaf to the back so that they stick out just enough.

2 With black embroidery thread and using a back stitch (page 124), stitch the facial features and berry lines. Use a blanket stitch (page 124) and matching thread to sew the two head pieces together.

3 Hot-glue the hair comb to the back of the felt shape so the teeth of the comb stick out from the bottom.

I suspect that I've been targeted by the Guild of Assassins.

CHAPTER 3

Give me a hug, hero.

RHOMBUS HOME DECOR

Whether you live in a castle, a cave, or a tree fort, your house should be a place to relax and hang out. The projects and ideas in this chapter will certainly add spice and personality to turn your abode into a welcoming respite. Or surprise someone with one of these homemade projects from the heart. Best housewarming present ever!

As you master the skills to create these projects, you'll be a pioneer in making granny crafts cool again. Update an old-fashioned sampler for the kitchen. Stitch up a cozy throw pillow. Or what the stuff, get your crochet on! Just don't be shocked if Marceline tries to evict you, now that you've fixed up the place.

BMO'S 8-BIT FUSE BEAD COASTERS

One reason I love fuse beads is that they look just like retro video-game graphics. Straight-up BMO style! Maybe you thought that fuse beads (also known as Perler® or Hama beads) were just a kids' thing, but you'll find that there's so much you can do with them: make jewelry, hair bows, wall art, or these drink coasters. It's the most fun you'll *ever* have ironing.

YOU WILL NEED

BMO's 8-Bit Fuse Bead Coasters chart (page 137)

Fuse beads in various colors for each character:

- **Ice King:** white, yellow-orange, light blue, black, dark red, and red

- **Princess Bubblegum:** hot pink, light pink, yellow-orange, black, purple, and white

- **Marceline:** black, light gray, red, white, and pink

- **Finn:** tan, white, medium blue, lime green, dark red, pink, and black

- **Jake:** yellow-orange, black, white, orange, dark red, brown, and pink

- **BMO:** teal, light blue, white, black, blue, yellow, lime green, and red

Fuse bead pegboard, at least 4" x 4" (10cm x 10cm)

Iron

Ironing board

Parchment paper (see notes)

- Some packs of fuse beads will come with a sheet of parchment paper, but you can also find parchment paper at your local grocery store.

- Try making your own patterns at http://kandipatterns.com. Mark the bead type as "square" and start designing.

STEPS

1 Set the fuse bead pegboard on a flat surface. Following the 8-Bit Fuse Bead Coaster chart (page 137), place the beads on the corresponding pegs of the fuse board for one of the characters (A).

A

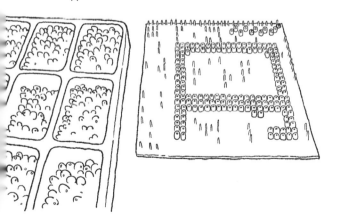

2 Once all the colors are placed, double-check the design to make sure all the beads are in the right spot and all the colors are correct. There's no going back after you iron! Carefully move the fuse bead pegboard to the ironing board.

3 This part's for adults only: Preheat the iron to medium heat and place the parchment paper on top of the beads. Before you iron, check that none of the beads have fallen off or wriggled loose. Gently iron the design in a circular motion, until the beads begin to fuse. This should only take about 10 to 20 seconds. Make sure you get those pesky edges, too (B).

B

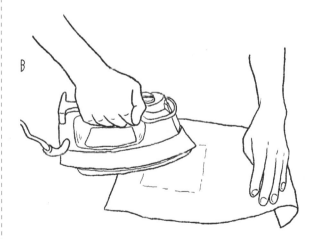

4 Wait for the first side to cool and carefully peel off the parchment paper. Take the beaded design off the pegboard, and flip it over onto the opposite side.

5 Repeat the process of placing and ironing beads for the entire chart until you've made all the characters, for a total of six coasters.

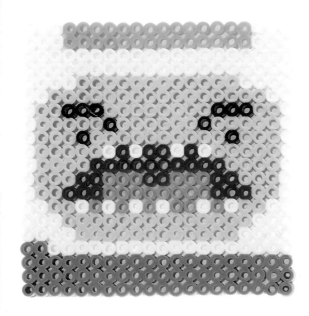

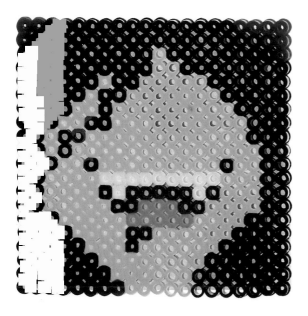

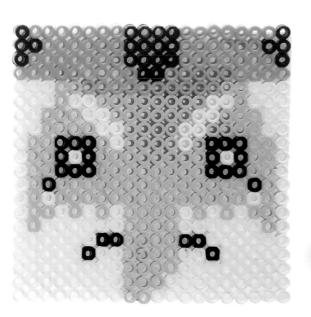

CRAFT PARTY PANIC!

I love to entertain, and a crafty get-together is the perfect excuse to turn on some jams and go crazy with your besties. Here are some of my favorite tips for hosting a totally math D.I.Y. party:

- Pick a relatively easy project to do together. Your guests may have different skill levels, and most people like to finish a craft that they can take home with them. The Fan Fiction Finger Puppets and Stage (page 10), Princess Hair Adornments (page 60), and Shrink-a-Cow-Tastic Jewelry (page 42) are good projects for all abilities.

- Have a clothing swap! Ask guests to each bring at least one item of clothing in good condition that they no longer wear. With a little paint or a stitched embellishment, you can turn that boring sweater or old pair of sneakers into a chic fashion statement.

- Set up a nail art bar with a few shades of polish and striping brushes. If your friends finish their craft projects early, they can do their nails, too! Check out Chalkboard Nails's tutorial for Oh My Glob, Nail Art! (page 56) for inspiration.

JAKE'S BACON PANCAKES WALL ART

Like you even needed an excuse to make bacon pancakes. This appliquéd wall art will inspire you to sing Jake's pancake song while you cook up the tastiest treat ever invented by a magical dog.

A sharp pair of detail scissors will help the appliqués look neat and crisp. If you're confident with your freehand scissor skills, you can add other breakfast foods on the counter in front of Jake. Hey, it's never too early for an everything burrito.

YOU WILL NEED

Jake's Bacon Pancakes Wall Art template (page 138)

Scissors

8" (20.5cm) embroidery hoop

Light-colored cotton fabric, at least 10" x 10" (25.5cm x 25.5cm)

Felt in yellow-orange, light gray, dark gray, red, pink, black, white

Embroidery floss in a color that contrasts with the background fabric, plus black

Sewing thread to match felt colors, plus black

Sewing needle

Pins

Embroidery needles

Hot-glue gun

Tailor's chalk or water-soluble fabric pen

Bacon pancakes, makin' bacon pancakes.
Take some bacon and I'll put it in a pancake.
Bacon pancakes, that's what I'm gonna make.
Bacon pancaaaaakes!

STEPS

1 Trace the template (page 138), and cut out the pattern pieces, cutting out the words together as one big piece and setting that aside.

2 Use the pattern pieces to cut out the appliqué shapes from felt, in corresponding colors following the photo (A).

3 Pull the background fabric taut inside the embroidery hoop. Trim the overhanging fabric, leaving about 1" (2.5cm) excess all the way around.

4 Pin down the big pieces (counter, Jake's body pieces, and the pan) and appliqué them to the background fabric with matching sewing thread and a running stitch (page 127), pulling the thread taut as you go. Then appliqué the smaller detail pieces, including Jake's mouth pieces, the pan interior, and the bacon (B).

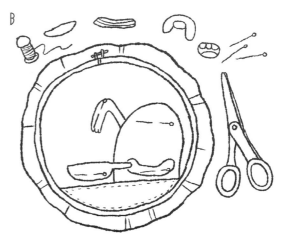

5 Using black sewing thread and a back stitch (page 124), embroider the lip around the pan, following the photo.

6   With the tailor's chalk or a water-soluble fabric pen, lightly mark the lines for Jake's eyes and ear, plus the heat lines on the background fabric. Embroider the lines using black embroidery floss and a back stitch. Double the embroidery thread when stitching the eyes so they pop more (C).

C

7   Pin the pattern piece with the song lyrics to the background fabric, centering it in the empty space above Jake. Using the contrasting-colored floss and a back stitch, sew through the paper following the lines of the letters.

8   Once all the words are embroidered, slowly and carefully rip out the paper from underneath it. Use a pin to pull out the small pieces that are stuck (D).

D

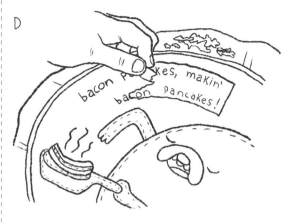

9   Hot-glue the excess background fabric around the hoop to the inside edges.

You're gonna be my breakfast baby.

You're gonna be my brunch!

PEPPERMINT BUTLER PILLOW

Normally, you wouldn't want to fall asleep on a giant piece of hard candy, but this big, squishy version of Peps is a total softie. Check out his coattails! Everyone loves giant, oversized pillows, so I made this pillow pretty large and in charge. But if you want a customized decoration, simply scale the template to make the pillow details whatever size you want.

Either way, Peppermint Butler will make a loyal and delicious addition to your couch or bedside. For an ecofriendly option, consider stuffing him with fabric scraps left over from other sewing projects.

YOU WILL NEED

Peppermint Butler Pillow templates (page 139)

White fleece, at least two pieces that are 16" x 16" (40.5cm x 40.5cm) or larger

Felt in red, blue, yellow, black, and white

Embroidery thread in black

Embroidery thread in colors that match the felt pieces

Sewing needles

Sewing pins

Stuffing or fabric scraps

Pen or tailor's chalk

Sewing machine (optional)

NOTE: If you don't have a sewing machine, don't worry! You can sew this entire project by hand with a running stitch (page 127) or back stitch (page 124). I prefer a back stitch because it adds extra reinforcement.

Fine craftsmanship, milady!

STEPS

1 Cut two equal circles, 16" in diameter, out of the white fleece. These pieces will be the front and back of Peppermint Butler's body. Then cut out the other shapes following the templates (page 139), enlarged 200 percent for a pillow 16" in diameter. There are a total of 14 peppermint stripes, 4 eye pieces, 4 buttons in black and yellow, 2 waistcoat fronts, and 2 coattail pieces.

2 Pin the waistcoat fronts a little below the center of the white body pieces. Make sure they match up on both sides, and the bottom of the V in the waistcoat is centered with a straight line down the front of the body.

3 Place one of the peppermint stripes on either side just above the top line of the blue waistcoat, and one in the top center (A). Pin down and then arrange two more between them so they're all equidistant from one another. Repeat on the back side, making sure that the stripes match up with their corresponding front pieces.

A

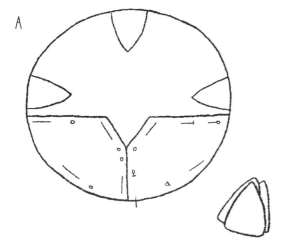

4 Arrange the eye pieces, with the white circle on top of the black circle near the center of the pillow. Pin them down with small pins. With a pen or pencil, *lightly* mark a line for Peps's mouth. The sample pillow has a simple straight line for the mouth, but you could give him a little smile or frown instead. With black embroidery floss and a back stitch (page 124), embroider the mouth following the drawn line (B).

B

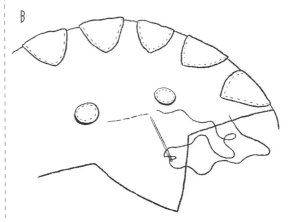

5 With matching thread, sew the white part of the eyes in place, attaching them to the white fleece background. Leave the black circles alone so the eyes stick out a bit.

6 With a sewing machine or by hand, sew the peppermint stripes in place with red thread. Make sure each stripe is lined up with its corresponding stripe on the back piece.

7 Using a sewing machine or by hand, stitch down the waistcoat fronts, making sure that the edges on both sides line up.

8   To make the bow tie, cut two strips of red felt, one 2" x 9" (5cm x 23cm) and one 1" x 2½" (2.5cm x 6.5cm). Fold one side of the long strip about two-thirds of the way in, and then fold the rest over it so the strip is folded in three equal sections. Pinch it in the center, and then wrap the smaller piece of felt around the center tightly, pinning the ends in the back. Stitch the ends together.

9   Sew the finished bow tie onto the body piece in between the V in the waistcoat. Make several stitches on either side into the crease of the bow. Then stitch the two little black button shapes under the bow tie.

10 Sew the yellow button pieces onto one coattail piece. Then pin the two coattail pieces right sides facing each other, and run this through the machine, leaving the top side open. Snip the corners off the ends without cutting through the stitches, and cut a notch in the V between them. Turn the tail right side out, using something like a pencil tip or a chopstick to poke the pointy ends out. Pin the tail onto Peppermint Butler's butt of the pants and sew the open top piece in place (C).

11 Now you have all the body pieces done! Pin the tail piece up, so it's away from the edge. Place the finished body pieces right side facing each other, and pin along the edges. Make sure to carefully line up all the stripes and pant lines together.

12 With a ¼" (6mm) seam allowance, sew around the perimeter of the pillow, leaving a hole that you can fit your hand in to flip it through. Turn the pillow right side out through the hole, and push along the edges to make them look smooth. Unpin the tail from the back.

13 Stuff it! I like polyester fiberfill, but you can use fabric scraps to fill it up instead. This option gives the pillow a bit more weight, and also makes it ecofriendly.

14 Close up the hole in a matching thread color, hiding your stitches. Time to snuggle up with your new buddy!

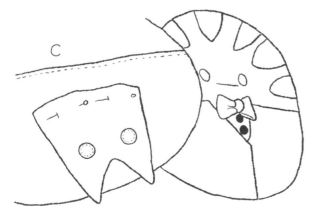

ADVENTURE TIP
If you don't feel proficient enough with embroidery you could make a mouth out of a thin strip of black felt instead. A fabric marker or fabric paint will also get the job done.

LEMONGRAB'S UNWELCOME! MAT

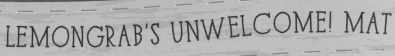

Since Lemongrab's not exactly a fan of people dropping by, I made this doormat to help him add "lemon styles" to his castle. The design is created with three layers of stencils to create a multicolor image, and then details are added with fabric paint and a brush. Go outdoors, because you'll need fresh air and space to work with the stencils and spray paint.

YOU WILL NEED

Lemongrab's Unwelcome! Mat templates (page 140)

Doormat in a solid color

Spray paint in white, yellow, and black

Fabric paint in white and black

Bristol board, poster board, or thick paper

Paintbrushes

Painter's tape

Craft knife

Pencil or pen

STEPS

1   Cut out Lemongrab's head from the template
    (page 140) with the craft knife. I used Bristol
    board, but you can use poster board, card
    stock, or thick paper. Cut out the head shape
    and use the leftover board to make the eye
    stencil. Trace the head shape again to cut
    out the black shapes: the pupil, nose line,
    and mouth. You will have three stencils in
    total (A).

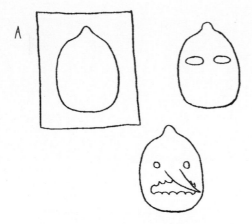

A

2   Place the first stencil (the outline of
    Lemongrab's head) on the doormat. I chose
    to put mine in the top middle, but aligning it
    left is also a good choice. Remember to leave
    space for the letters. Tape the stencil down
    with painter's tape. If you think you'll be really
    messy, cover the rest of the doormat with
    paper. I put a couple of heavy things around
    my stencil to make sure it was lying flat (B).

3   Prime the shape first with white spray
    paint. Paint one or two coats of the white,
    sweeping it across the stencil holding it
    straight down about 6" (15cm) from the
    design.

4   Spray several coats of yellow on top of the
    white, waiting a few minutes in between
    each coat. The darker the color of the
    doormat, the more coats it will take to get a
    nice yellow color.

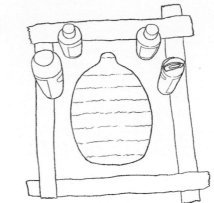

B

5   Once the yellow paint is dry, peel off the
    stencil. Then place the eye stencil on top of
    the yellow silhouette, and tape down. Spray a
    few coats of white spray paint, and wait for it
    to dry.

6   While you're waiting, trace the word
    "UNWELCOME" onto card stock and cut it
    out with a craft knife. If the word spans more
    than one page of paper, tape multiple sheets
    of paper together.

7 Center the word underneath Lemongrab's head, tape the stencil down, and place paper around it to cover the edge of the mat. I put little rolled-up pieces of tape underneath the skinnier parts of the letters, and for the center of the "O," to ensure they'd stay in place (C).

C

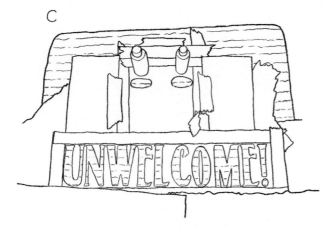

8 Spray the letters with the white paint in long sweeping motions. Do a few coats, and then wait for the paint to dry. I wanted my exclamation point to be yellow, so I blocked off the other letters, and sprayed it with yellow paint a few times.

9 When the letters have dried, peel the stencil off. If the letters aren't as nice in the grooves as you'd like, you can touch up the edges with white fabric paint, and use black fabric paint (or whatever color matches the doormat) to crisp up the lines around Lemongrab's head and the letters.

10 Tape the last stencil (the one with the pupils and mouth) down over the face, making sure to line up the pupil with the whites of the eyes. Cover the rest of the doormat with paper and spray over the stencil. Do a few coats and wait for it to dry. Then carefully peel the stencil off.

11 With a paintbrush and white fabric paint, fill in the teeth, and then paint, and then add the inside of the mouth with black fabric paint. Wait for the doormat to fully dry before using. You don't want to stomp paint all over the castle, ya big butt!

If you don't try your hand at making this craft, I find that unacceptable! Ten years dungeon!

CROCHET HOMIES COZIES BY YUMMY PANCAKE

Are you and your best bud as tight as Finn and Jake? Then you need a pair of these sweet drink cozies, made with basic crochet techniques. They are perfect for protecting your can of bug milk, honey energy drink, or whatever type of liquid goodness you choose. If you prefer a beverage from the Breakfast Kingdom as your fuel, this pattern also offers instructions to make matching coffee cozies.

YOU WILL NEED

Size G-6 (4mm) crochet hook

Worsted-weight yarn (Red Heart Super Saver)

- **Finn:** 24 yards (22m) each in teal and white
- **Jake:** 54 yards (49.5m) in gold, 7 yards (6.5m) each in white and black

Yarn needle

FINN COZY ONLY

2" x 2½" (5cm x 6.5cm) rectangle of felt in peach

Hot-glue gun and sticks

Fabric paint in black, pearlescent white (optional), and glitter red (optional)

JAKE COZY ONLY

Polyester fiberfill

NOTES

• Worsted-weight yarn is also known as medium-weight yarn. Most worsted-weight yarns will be labeled with this symbol: 🧶4️⃣

• For illustrations and descriptions of all the crochet stitches used to make these cozies, turn to Crafty Basics (page 124).

ABBREVIATIONS

CH	chain stitch
DEC	decrease
HDC	half double crochet
SC	single crochet
ST	stitch

GAUGE

4 sts and 4 rows = 1" (2.5cm) over pattern stitch

FINN CAN COZY

EARS (MAKE 2)

With white yarn, ch 5, 1 sc in 2nd chain from hook, 1 sc in next 2 chains, 3 sc in next chain.

Now, down the other side of the original chain of 5, 1 sc in each chain.

Finish off, leaving a long tail to sew onto the can cozy.

BODY

Round 1: With teal yarn, ch 2, 6 sc in 2nd single crochet from hook (6).

Round 2: 2 sc in each stitch (12).

Round 3: * 1 sc, 2 sc in next stitch, repeat from * around (18).

Round 4: *(1 sc) two times, 2 sc in next stitch, repeat from * around (24).

Round 5: *(1 sc) three times, 2 sc in next stitch, repeat from * around (30).

Round 6: *(1 sc) four times, 2 sc in next stitch, repeat from * around (36).

Round 7: In back stitch, 1 sc around (36).

Rounds 8–13: 1 sc in each stitch (36).

Round 14: Change to white yarn, 1 sc in each stitch (36).

Round 15: 1 sc in each stitch (36).

NOTE: The following instructions are for crocheting in rows instead of rounds to create an opening for Finn's face.

Row 16: 1 sc in first 15 stitches, ch 1, turn.

Row 17: Dec across first 2 stitches, 1 sc in next 28 stitches, ch 1, turn (29).

Row 18: Dec across first 2 stitches, 1 sc in next 27 stitch, ch 1, turn (28).

Row 19: 2 sc in first stitch, 1 sc in next 27 stitches, ch 1, turn (29).

Row 20: 2 sc in first stitch, 1 sc in next 28 stitches, ch 1, turn (30).

NOTE: Now go back to crocheting in rounds in order to close up Finn's face opening.

Round 21: 2 sc in first stitch, 1 sc in next 28 stitches, ch 6, 1 sc in next 15 stitches (on the other side of the face opening).

Round 22: 1 sc in first 15 stitches, 6 sc in ch 6 split from last step, 1 sc in next 15 stitches (36).

Finish off, weaving in the end of the yarn.

FINISHING

Sew the ears onto the cozy as pictured.

Glue the piece of peach felt on the face opening using the hot-glue gun. With the fabric paint, draw a face onto the felt.

Finn Coffee Cozy Modification Would you rather make a cozy for a coffee cup instead of a can? No problem! Here's how to modify this pattern:

Round 1: With white yarn, ch 36, join with first chain to form a ring.

Round 2: 1 sc in each chain around (36).

Now, continue from Round 15 of Finn Can Cozy pattern.

JAKE CAN COZY

EARS (MAKE 2)

With gold yarn, ch 5, 1 sc in 2nd chain from hook, 1 sc in next 5 chains, 3 sc in next chain.

Now, down the other side of the original chain of 8, 1 sc in each chain.

Finish off, leaving a long tail to sew onto the can cozy.

OUTER EYES (MAKE 2)

Round 1: With black yarn, ch 2, 6 sc in 2nd single crochet from hook (6).

Round 2: 2 sc in each stitch (12).

Finish off, leaving a long tail to sew onto the can cozy.

INNER EYES (MAKE 2)

Round 1: With white yarn, ch 2, 5 sc in 2nd single crochet from hook (5).

Round 2: 2 sc in each stitch (10).

Finish off, leaving a long tail to sew onto the can cozy.

ADVENTURE TIP
Get creative with Finn's facial expressions! You don't need to follow the photo. Fabric paint is a quick and easy solution, but feel free to use embroidery floss and a back stitch (page 124) if you are making a simpler face.

NOSE

With black yarn, ch 4, 1 sc in 2nd chain from hook, 1 sc in next chain, 3 sc in next chain.

Now, down the other side of the original chain of 4, 1 sc in next chain, 2 sc in next chain.

Finish off, leaving a long tail to sew onto the can cozy.

SNOUT

Round 1: With gold yarn, ch 2, 6 sc in 2nd single crochet from hook (6).

Round 2: *(1 sc) two times, 2 sc in next stitch, repeat from * around (8).

Rounds 5–7: 1 sc in each stitch (8).

Rounds 8–9: 1 sc, 1 slip stitch in next 3 stitches, 1 sc, 1 hdc in next 3 stitches (8).

Rounds 10–14: 1 sc in each stitch (8).

NOTE: Stop here, and fill the snout with polyester fiberfill before you continue.

Round 15: *(1 sc) two times, dec across next 2 stitches, repeat from * around (6).

Finish off, leaving a long tail to sew onto the can cozy.

CAN COZY

Round 1: With gold yarn, ch 2, 6 sc in 2nd single crochet from hook (6).

Round 2: 2 sc in each stitch (12).

Round 3: * 1 sc, 2 sc in next stitch, repeat from * around (18).

Round 4: *(1 sc) two times, 2 sc in next stitch, repeat from * around (24).

Round 5: *(1 sc) three times, 2 sc in next stitch, repeat from * around (30).

Round 6: *(1 sc) four times, 2 sc in next stitch, repeat from * around (36).

Round 7: In back stitch, 1 sc around (36).

Rounds 8–24: 1 sc in each stitch (36).

Finish off, weaving in the end of the yarn.

I can shake-a my fanny!

I can shake-a my can!

FINISHING

Sew the black outer eyes onto the can cozy, and then sew the white inner eyes onto the black outer eyes.

Sew the snout onto the cozy, and then sew the nose onto the snout. With black yarn, embroider the mouth.

Sew on each ear.

Jake Coffee Cozy Modification
As with the complementary Finn cozy, this pattern easily converts into a coffee cup cozy, with these minor alterations:

Round 1: With gold yarn, ch 36, join with first chain to form a ring.

Round 2: 1 sc in each chain around (36).

Now, continue from Round 15 of the Jake Can Cozy pattern.

(Soda) Pop Quiz!

Whatcha gonna use your cozy for? Finn and Jake like to be the hosts with the most, so they keep everyone's favorite drinks on hand for Finn and Jake Movie Club. Test how well you know their friends by matching each character to his or her preferred beverage. (Check your answers at the bottom of the page!)

1. Lady Rainicorn
2. Lumpy Space Princess
3. Tree Trunks
4. BMO
5. Marceline

a. apple juice
b. iced latte
c. hot cocoa
d. diet soda
e. tomato juice

Answers: 1 b, 2 d, 3 a, 4 c, 5 e

CHAPTER 4

What the plum are you wearing? You look horrible!

GEEK CHIC FASHION

Style is very personal in the Land of Ooo. Some kids like to wear the same white hat day in and day out. Other citizens don't wear any clothes at all! Personally, I enjoy dressing up and having fun with fashion, and I hope you'll find something in this section of the book that suits your style, too.

The accessories in this chapter will stretch your sewing skills and build on techniques from earlier sections of the book. Learn how to create a custom-fit skirt, sew from patterns, and even insert linings. But not everything must be made from scratch! With a little bit of paint and simple embellishment techniques, you can add a handmade touch to store-bought items or even upcycle garments from your own wardrobe.

FIONNA AND FINN HATS

Every hero needs a hat to keep his or her head warm and long, flowing locks under control. Finn's practical hat is his most recognizable accessory, so here's the pattern and instructions to make your own.

Fleece is easy to sew because it doesn't need to be hemmed like other fabrics. The hat could be sewn all in one fabric, but I like to make the lining in felt and use soft fleece for the exterior. And of course, feel free to switch the bear ears with long rabbit ears to make a girlier version.

YOU WILL NEED

Fionna and Finn Hats templates (page 141)

White fleece, at least 35" x 12" (89cm x 30.5cm)

White felt, at least 35" x 12" (89cm x 30.5cm)

Scissors

Sewing machine

Sewing needle and thread

Tailor's chalk or water-soluble fabric pen

Stuffing

Velcro™

Hot-glue gun (optional)

Fire the laser cannon!

A

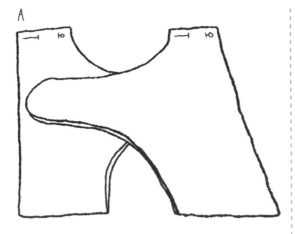

B

C

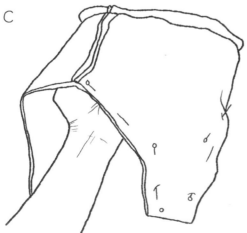

STEPS

1 Trace the templates (page 141), and cut out the felt and fleece pieces as follows: Cut one pair of ears out of fleece, cut two circle pieces (one felt, one fleece), and two brim pieces (one felt, one fleece).

2 Sew the short ends of the fleece brim together. Repeat for the felt brim piece (A).

3 Pin the circle around the brim top. Sew the right sides together on both fleece and felt.

4 Pin the fleece ears right side together and run through the machine, leaving them open at the bottom. Turn the ears right side out, lightly stuff, and sew closed.

5 With tailor's chalk or a water-soluble fabric pen, mark the width of the ears on the top of the fleece section of the hat. Cut slits where the ears will be placed, and insert the ears into the slits. Sew the ears onto the fleece hat on the inside (B).

6 Place the felt and fleece hat pieces right sides together, and pin. Run the edges through the sewing machine, leaving a hole in the back to flip (C).

7 Flip the hat right side out and push the felt side into the fleece side. Close the hole with a ladder stitch.

8 Cut two small pieces of Velcro and either sew or hot-glue them to the left side of each earflap.

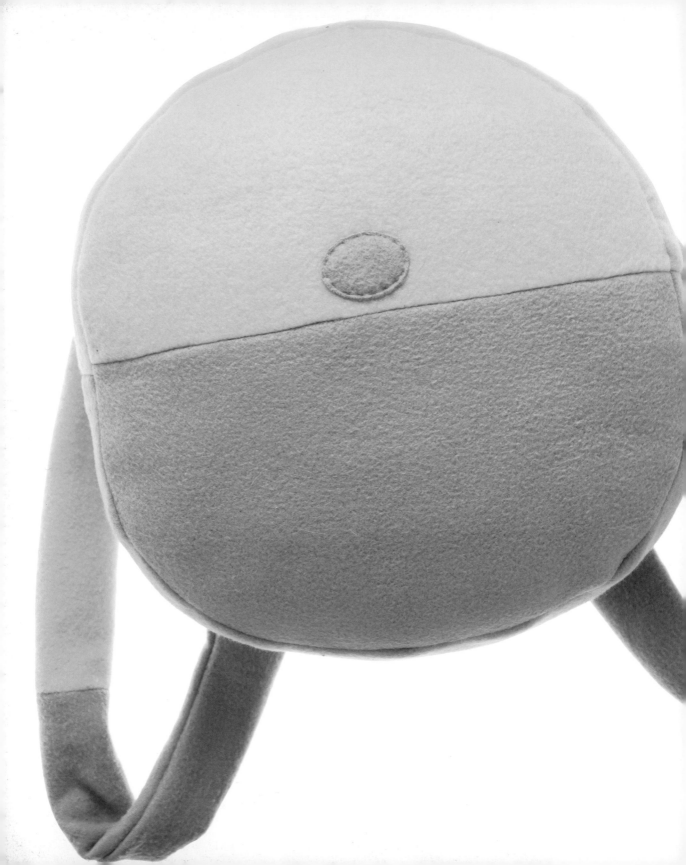

RIGHTEOUS HERO BACKPACK

What kind of adventurer would you be without a pack? I mean, where would you stash your sword? (Or for that matter, marshmallows, tape, your friend's snow booties, and all the other junk that Finn carries around.) Pair your hat (page 94) with a blue shirt and shorts or a skirt, and you'll look just like your favorite hero.

This project can be made with a closure, such as Velcro or a zipper, to make it a usable backpack. But you can skip that step and still end up with a pretty sweet costume accessory or a travel pillow for adventurous picnics.

YOU WILL NEED

Fleece, at least 30" x 22" (76cm x 56cm) each in dark green and light green

Sewing machine

Sewing needle and thread

Scissors

Polyester fiberfill (optional)

Zipper or Velcro (optional)

A

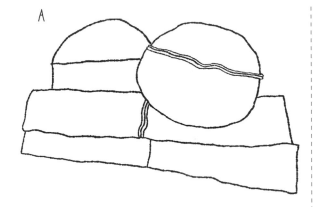

B

C

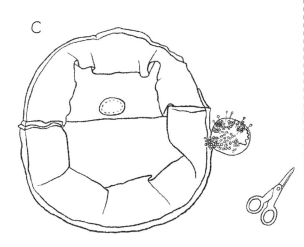

STEPS

1 Cut out the pattern pieces. The pack is made out of supersimple shapes that you can measure directly onto the fleece. You'll need the following pieces: one small dark green oval; two half-oval pieces in light green, about 7" (18cm) tall x 14" (35.5cm) across; two half-oval pieces in dark green about 8" (20.5cm) tall x 14" (35.5cm) across; one long strip of light green 3½" x 22" (9cm x 56cm), and one dark green 3½" x 24" (9cm x 61cm); and two rectangles in light green and two rectangles in dark green, each 5½" x 16" (14cm x 40.5cm). (These last four pieces are for the straps and can be trimmed down later based on your height.)

2 Pin the light green half-oval pieces to the dark green pieces along the straight edges and sew together. Appliqué the small dark green oval to one of the light green half-ovals, following the photo (page 98).

3 Pin the short edge of a light green rectangle (5½" x 16" [14cm x 40.5cm]) to the corresponding dark green rectangle, and sew together. Repeat with the second pair of light/dark green 5½" x 16" (14cm x 40.5cm) rectangles (A).

4 Fold each of the straps in half lengthwise, right sides together. Pin and sew down the long edge, leaving the ends open. Turn right side out.

5 Place the straps on top of the backpack shape and mark where they will go. Cut slits into the fabric, two on top and two on the bottom, making sure they're lined up with each other.

Push the straps through the slits in their corresponding colors. Pin and try on to see if the backpack is the correct length for your body. Pull more through to the back if the straps are too long. Sew the straps in place on the back side of the backpack shape (B).

6 Pin the 3½" x 22" (9cm x 56cm) piece of light green fleece along the corresponding perimeter of the half-oval piece. Do the same with the long strip of dark green fleece, and pin the ends of the long strips together. Run through the machine (C).

7 Pin the two backpack pieces right sides together, and sew around the perimeter, leaving an opening big enough for your hand to fit through. Make sure to push the straps inside so they do not get caught in the line of stitching.

8 Turn the backpack right side out through the gap that you left. At this step, you can choose to make the pack functional by adding a zipper, Velcro, or snaps to the opening.

9 For a prop backpack (or a ginormous travel pillow), stuff with polyester fiberfill through the hole, pushing toward the edges so it doesn't come out looking wiggly. Stuff until it looks nice and round, just like Finn's backpack.

Schmow-zow! I'll slay anything that's evil. That's my deal!

HOT LIKE PIZZA SUPPER SKIRT

I love fun, colorful skirts! This skater style would be perfect for spinning across the ballroom floor of the Candy Castle while doing the science dance with Finn.

Thanks to the elastic waistband and a foolproof mathematical formula (see Step 1), it's entirely customizable to your own body measurements. Pair this skirt with sandals in the summer, or with warm leggings and cute boots when the weather gets cooler.

YOU WILL NEED

1½ yards (1.5m) of fabric (or more depending on your desired length)

2" (5cm) wide elastic (see Step 6)

Scissors

Tape measure

Sewing machine

Thread

Tailor's chalk

Paper and pencil (optional)

Iron and ironing board

NOTES:

- The radius of a circle is the measurement from the center point to the edge of the circle. In this project you are using the measuring tape as a compass to create a circle with a radius that matches your waist circumference.

- For Steps 3 and 4, you can use a large sheet of paper (or smaller sheets taped together) to make a pattern first. Or mark directly on your fabric, as shown in the steps.

STEPS

1 Measure around your waist, where it creases when you bend to the side. Add 2" (5cm) to that measurement, and divide it by 6.28. This measurement will be the radius of the skirt.

2 Fold the fabric into fourths, with the wrong side facing out.

3 Using a measuring tape and tailor's chalk, and starting from the corner of the folded fabric, mark a point along the edge of the fabric that equals the radius measurement. Mark several points and connect them to create a quarter of the skirt.

4 Place your tape measure around the outside of the quarter circle you just marked, and mark out the skirt length. I wanted mine to be cute and short, so it is 17" (43cm) long, but you can make it longer if you wish. It's best to leave a bit extra in case you decide to cut some off at the end, and don't forget to factor in the added length of the waistband width (A).

5 Now carefully cut out the pattern, first cutting out the small ¼ circle and then the big circle, following the lines marked in Steps 3 and 4. Set the fabric aside (B).

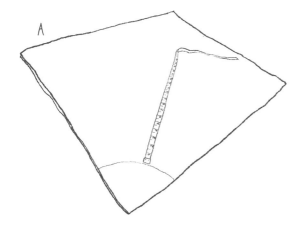

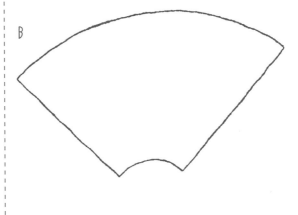

6 Cut a length of elastic 1" (2.5cm) longer than your natural waist measurement.

7 Fold the elastic in half, pin, and sew ends together, with a ½" (13mm) seam allowance. Then fan out the ends and sew them down flat. The finished elastic band should be slightly smaller than the waistband of the fabric. Give it a check on your waist to make sure it's the right fit before moving to the next step.

8 Starting from the middle back of the skirt, begin to pin the elastic about ¼" (6mm) into the waistband of the skirt. Then flip it over and pin it to the middle front. After that, pin the elastic down on the far right and left sides of the skirt. Then fill up the gaps with as many pins as you're comfortable with to sew it down (C).

9 Now it's time to sew the elastic to the fabric. Use a corresponding colored thread with your elastic, and pull the elastic taut onto the skirt as you go. Straight stitch or zigzag stitch both look good with this.

10 Now try it on! If you're happy with the length, just make sure it looks even all the way around and trim the edge if necessary.

11 Fold the bottom of the skirt by ¼" (6mm), press with an iron, and pin down. Straight stitch the edge to hem the skirt.

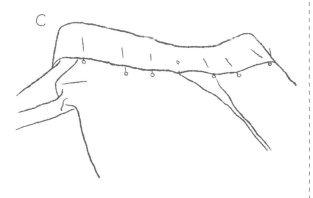

C

She's red hot like pizza supper.

ADVENTURE TIP
When matching thread to a sewing project, lay a length of thread across the fabric to see how it will look. If the fabric has a print like this one, match the thread to the background color.

TREE TRUNKS'S PAINTED KICKS
BY PONY CHOPS SHOP

Going on an adventure? Well, I have the perfect thing for you . . . new shoes! And not just any shoes. These custom-painted slip-ons feature Tree Trunks, the sweetest little pie-making elephant in the Candy Kingdom.

Use this same technique to transfer any piece of fan art to your feet. It takes some practice, but the nice thing about acrylics is that if you make a mistake, you can just wait for the boo-boo to dry and paint over it.

YOU WILL NEED

Acrylic paints in lime green, white, bubblegum pink, and red (see notes)

Paintbrushes

Pencil

Glass of water

White canvas shoes

Permanent black marker pen (Faber-Castell)

Acrylic waterproof spray (optional)

NOTES:

- Tree Trunks's shoes were painted with Liquitex Brilliant Yellow Green, System 3 White, Liquitex Magenta, and Liquitex Cadmium Red.

- The glass of water is to rinse out your brush between colors, silly!

I baked y'all an apple pie!

ADVENTURE TIP

Any blank white canvas shoe will work with acrylics. Try decking out a pair of sneakers (just remove the laces first) or even a pair of blank high heels. I can't wait to see the crazy combinations you dream up!

STEPS

1 Paint the top and front of the shoes in pastel lime green. The color in the sample project was achieved by mixing Liquitex Brilliant Yellow Green with white.

2 Paint the back of the shoes in bubblegum pink. The color in the sample project was achieved by mixing Liquitex Magenta with white. Wait for the shoes to dry completely.

3 With a pencil, carefully draw Tree Trunks's trunk, starting at the center of the shoe. Imagine her trunk as a "J" with a little heart shape on the end.

4 On either side of the top of the trunk, draw a circle for Tree Trunks's eyes. Draw two little circles inside each eye.

5 Draw Tree Trunks's mouth, adding extra outlines for her teeth and tongue.

6 Sketch her wrinkles: one on the top and bottom of each eye, two on her forehead, and two on her trunk.

7 Mix a slightly darker lime green, and use it to paint around the edges of her face, on her wrinkles and down one edge of the trunk.

8 Fill in the details. Paint her tongue pink, her teeth white, and the two little circles in her eyes white. Then add some black paint or marker pen to the inside of her mouth and eyes.

9 With a permanent marker, trace over the pencil lines to emphasize the facial details.

10 Add some white highlights to the edge of her trunk and next to the wrinkles.

11 Sketch a little red apple on the back of each heel and fill in the shape with red paint. Trace the outline with permanent marker.

BMO PHONE AND TABLET CASES

Finn and Jake's video-game console, BMO, invented a game called "Conversation Parade" that inspired this easy-to-sew project. Sadly, these BMOs are not playable . . . but if you take your sweet time, some of your friends may think that they are!

You can alter the dimensions to fit your phone, tablet, or even a portable video-game player!

NOTE: The amount of felt needed will depend on the size of the phone or other device. The large case used 2 pieces, 14" x 11" (35.5cm x 28cm) and 14" x 16" (35.5cm x 40.5cm). If you have extra felt lying around, you can use it in place of batting for the tablet case.

YOU WILL NEED

BMO Phone and Tablet Cases templates (page 142)

Felt in blue, dark blue, lime green, red, and yellow

Ruler or measuring tape

Printed cotton fabric

Matching embroidery thread

Scissors

Sewing thread and needle

Tailor's chalk or water-soluble marking pen

FOR PHONE CASE ONLY

One button

FOR TABLET CASE ONLY

Batting (optional)

Iron (optional)

Sew-on snap

Sewing machine

Black embroidery thread and needle

BMO PHONE CASE STEPS

1 Measure your phone, and then cut two long rectangles, one out of blue felt and one out of cotton fabric, about two and a half times the length of the phone and about ⅛" (3mm) wider on the sides. Cut two rounded corners on one of the short sides, on both fabrics.

2 Fold up the felt piece over your phone to see where the front will be. Leave approximately 3" (7.5cm) on the top front overhanging, which will form the flap. Mark the top and bottom of where the phone lies. This will be the front of BMO's face and body.

3 Using the templates (page 142), cut out all of BMO's face details and buttons in corresponding colors of felt. Appliqué the pieces to the blue felt, being mindful of the marks you made for the front of the phone case (A).

A

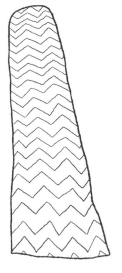

B

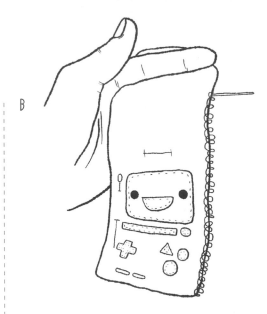

4 Place the cotton fabric with the wrong side up, and place the appliquéd felt piece right side up on top. Fold up into the case shape and pin the sides. With embroidery floss, blanket stitch (page 124) the edges of the two sides and flap. Don't forget the edge of the opening as well (B)!

5 Place the button on the back flap where you want it to lie and using tailor's chalk or a pencil, mark either side. Carefully use scissors to cut a slit into the flap. Use a running stitch (page 127) and embroidery floss to sew the felt and cotton fabric together at the slit. Trim off any fraying pieces of cotton fabric.

6 Place the button on the pocket side of the case underneath where the buttonhole is and sew down. Put your phone in the case, and button it closed.

Battery low. Shutdown.

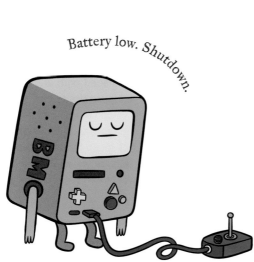

BMO TABLET CASE STEPS

1 Measure your tablet or laptop (or other electronic device), and cut two rectangles of blue felt ½" (13mm) wider and ½" (13mm) longer than the device. Cut a third rectangle of printed cotton fabric to these dimensions, and a fourth rectangle in batting or felt (see note after materials list).

2 Pin one rectangle of blue felt to the leftover printed cotton fabric. Create a house shape by cutting along the bottom and side lines to the dimensions of the blue felt rectangle and add a triangle to the top (the longer side) for the envelope flap. Round the pointed tip of the triangle off (C).

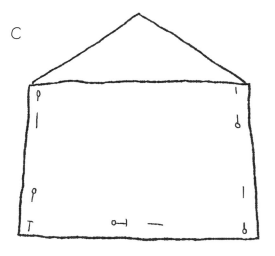

3 Use this house shape as a template to cut out two more shapes, one in the blue felt and one in the batting.

4 Arrange the three rectangles of fabric in this order: printed fabric with right side facing up, BMO felt, and batting. Pin the top (long) edge and run through the machine (D).

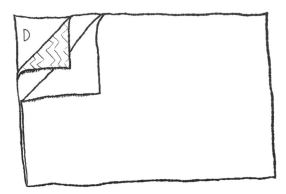

ADVENTURE TIP

The sew-on snap could be replaced with another type of closure pretty easily. Try using Velco (which can be sewn or glued on), a decorative button, or forgo the triangular flap altogether and install a zipper between two straight edges.

5 Flip the printed fabric over the batting. If you'd like, you can iron the edge on a low setting before you sew to make it a bit neater. Topstitch the edge—this is a straight line of stitching close to the edge that will be visible on the outside of the project.

6 Place your tablet in the center of the house-shaped piece of blue felt. Move the tablet up ½" (13mm) from the bottom and mark around it with tailor's chalk or water-soluble pen to mark the front of BMO's face and body.

7 Using the templates (page 142), cut out all of BMO's face details in their corresponding colors of felt. Pin and appliqué the felt details within the rectangle that you marked out. Depending on the size of the device, you may need to spread the facial details out a bit (E).

8 Cut a strand of black embroidery thread, double it over, and tie a knot at one end. Use tailor's chalk or a water-soluble pen to mark BMO's little smile, and follow these marks with the embroidery thread, using a back stitch (page 124).

9 Place the pieces in the following order: printed cotton fabric facing up, three sewn-together rectangular pieces (from Step 2) with the lining fabric facing down, BMO's face piece facing down, and the batting. Make sure all the pieces are lined up nicely and trim if there's a little excess.

10 Pin along the edges and run the stack of fabric through the machine, leaving a hole about 4" (10cm) wide in the top triangle piece (F).

E

F

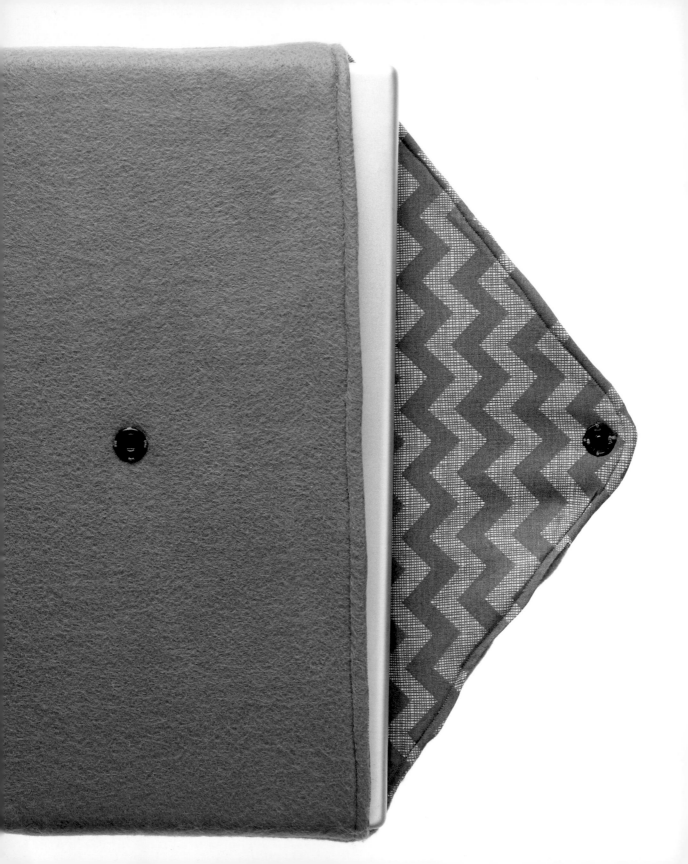

11 Turn right side out through the hole between the lining fabric and BMO face fabric. Push the edges and corners out with your finger, or use a chopstick to create nice crisp edges.

12 Turn the edges of the triangular tip in. Iron (if you want). Pin along the whole top triangle and topstitch.

13 Place the snaps (or Velcro or whatever closure you want) on the inside flap of the case. Hold the snap in place and neatly sew down by hand. Pull on the snap to make sure it's sewn down securely.

Press the flap down where the snap is to make an indent in the felt. This is where you'll sew the other snap. Hold the snap in place and securely sew down.

BMO chop!

BUBBLEGUM'S LIKE-LIKE SWEATER

If you're traveling to the Ice Kingdom or the Lich's lair, keep yourself warm with a slamacow sweater. If you make this customizable project for someone else, it will become enhanced with the powers of liking someone a lot, so he or she can defeat the most fearsome of villains.

The best thing about this project is that you don't need to know how to knit in order to make it! It looks like you have actually knit the design into the sweater when really you're only embellishing a store-bought sweater with a technique called duplicate stitch.

YOU WILL NEED

Bubblegum's Like-Like Sweater template (page 143)

Knitted sweater (see notes)

Yarn in contrasting color (see notes)

Yarn needle

Scissors

Iron

Towel

NOTES

- The sweater you buy (or make yourself) should be knit in plain stockinette stitch—that means the stitch pattern forms columns and rows of equally spaced V's and has a smooth surface.

- A chunky-knit sweater made with thicker yarn will make this project easier.

- Choose a contrasting color of yarn that is approximately the same thickness (or weight) as the yarn used in the sweater to make the motif.

ADVENTURE TIP

If you're feeling ambitious and have the skills to do so, you can knit a basic sweater yourself, and then add the duplicate stitched design. The same technique could also be applied to a knit beanie hat.

I'm not great at knitting,
but please wear it.
I *care* about you, Finn.

STEPS

1 Count the number of stitches in height and width in the template (page 143). Count the same amount on the sweater to see how large it will be, and determine where to place it. An asymmetrical composition means that you don't have to worry about centering the design. If you prefer the motif in the middle, place the sweater down flat and count out the sides to where the center mark is.

2 Thread a long length of yarn through the yarn needle, and triple-knot it at the end. Pull the yarn through the bottom of a stitch (at the base of the V shape) until it hits the knot. Pull the yarn across the V directly above the stitch you're working on (A).

A

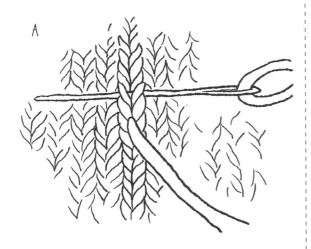

B

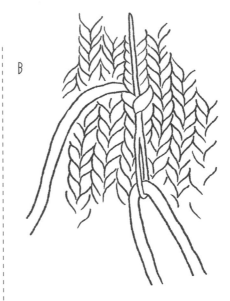

3 Now pull the yarn back down into the stitch you started from, creating one new V-shaped stitch in a contrasting color on top of the sweater stitch. Pull the yarn just enough so the yarn covers the stitch under it completely (B).

4 Move on to the next stitch, starting from its bottom point, across the stitch above it, and back down to its starting point.

C

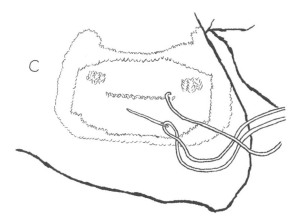

5 Create more duplicate stitches, first outlining the motif and then filling it in with stitches as indicated. If you make a mistake or you are unsatisfied with a stitch, pull it out using a pin and then rethread the yarn needle. When you run out of yarn on the needle, weave the tail into the stitches on the wrong side of the sweater (C).

6 Double-check your work by counting the stitches out from the sides of Finn's hat to make sure his eyes and mouth are centered in his face.

7 If you wish, add stripes to the sleeves or top of the collar. I added stripes on each sleeve five rows tall.

8 When your design is complete, dampen a towel and place it on top of the stitched areas of the sweater. With an iron on a low setting, press the face. (Be careful if you are using an acrylic yarn, which might melt.) Let it cool down before you try it on.

ADVENTURE TIP
You can make your own pattern using knitting graph paper, which has slightly wider squares than regular graph paper. Test this technique first by making a simple heart pattern with knitting graph paper, follow it on your sweater, and then adjust the template to make your pattern wider or taller to fit the stitch dimensions.

WHERE TO BUY STUFF

You don't need to spend a fortune on craft supplies. I tried to make these projects as inexpensive as possible, with alternative options for things you may already have around the house or can recycle. If you're having trouble finding a particular tool or material, turn to one of these tried and true sites.

Amazon
www.amazon.com
General art and craft supplies

Etsy
www.etsy.com
Search under "craft supplies"

Fabric.com
www.fabric.com
Sewing tools and materials

Hobby Lobby
www.hobbylobby.com
General craft supplies

Joann
www.joann.com
Fabric and sewing notions

Living Felt
www.livingfelt.com
Needle felting supplies, wool roving

Michaels Crafts
www.michaels.com
General craft supplies

D.I.Y. HEROES

These artists and designers did all the stitching, painting, crocheting, and other important labor to create the wonderful projects in this book. I implore you to please check out their websites and show some love for their creativity!

Chelsea Bloxsom
www.loveandasandwich.com

Chalkboard Nails
www.chalkboardnails.com

Pony Chops Shop
www.ponychops.co.uk

The Silvered Blade
www.etsy.com/shop/TheSilveredBlade

Yummy Pancake
www.etsy.com/shop/yummypancake

HELPFUL SITES

Here are some places around the Internet ether that I highly recommend, whether you are looking for more information about a craft technique or need inspiration to make your next project.

DeviantArt.com
This is a great place to share your finished works of art with other fans!

Etsy.com
In this online marketplace of handmade goods, you'll find thousands of products with *Adventure Time*™ tags. Hey, if you can't make it, buy it!

MakeZine.com
You'll find lots of helpful craft tutorials and cool geekery from around the D.I.Y. community.

YouTube.com
If you just can't seem to master a technique, search for an online video. I guarantee you that another crafter has created a helpful tutorial for that exact purpose.

To me, my penguins!

Gunter, Gunther, Gunder, Goonder, come on!

CRAFTY BASICS

These essential crafting techniques are used throughout the projects in this book. If you encounter a strange-looking term or need to refresh your memory, just look for it here. Some of these techniques will take a bit of time and patience to master, so don't worry if your first attempt doesn't turn out exactly like the finished project.

Back stitch

Use this stitch to create decorative embroidered lines on a piece of fabric *or* use it as a functional stitch when sewing by hand. Knot the end of the thread, and insert the needle from the back of the fabric to the front. Take the needle back about ⅛" (3mm), and insert through the fabric right to left, so that the needle point emerges about ⅛" (3mm) left of the knot. Continue working right to left to create a continuous line of stitching.

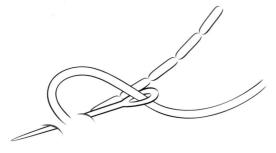

Blanket stitch

This is a great way to join two pieces of fabric along the edges. Stack two pieces of fabric. Knot the end of the thread and insert the needle from front to back of the top piece, hiding the knot in between the two pieces. Insert the needle through both pieces of fabric, about ¼" (6mm) from the raw edges and slightly to the right of the knot. Create a stitch perpendicular to the edge, and catch the needle over the loose loop. You will create a series of interlocking right angles for a decorative and functional edge.

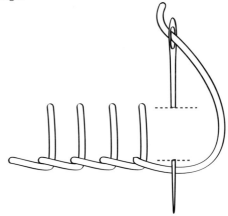

Dude, stinkin' at somethin' is the first step towards bein' sorta good at somethin'.

Chain stitch (crochet)

Start with a slip knot on the crochet hook. Wrap the working yarn over the crochet hook, from front to back. Slide the hook toward the slip knot, catching the yarn in the crook of the hood, and pull all the way through the slip knot.

Decrease (crochet)

Insert the crochet hook into the next stitch, as indicated in your pattern. Wrap the yarn around the hook and draw through the stitch. Work the next stitch in the same manner. You now have three loops on the hook. Wrap the yarn around the hook one more time and draw the yarn through all three of the loops on the hook.

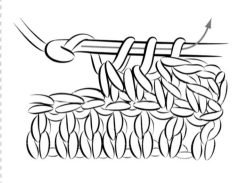

Do you think I've got the goods, Bubblegum? Because I am into this stuff!

French knot

You need to know this stitch to embroider little eyes for your creations! Knot the thread and insert the needle from back to front of the fabric. Wrap the thread twice around the tip of the needle as shown, and insert back through the needle. You will have a little knotted circle of thread on top of the fabric.

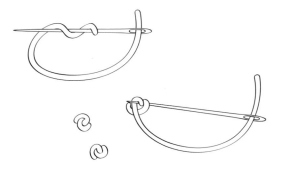

Ladder stitch

This hidden stitch is used to close toys, pillows, and other sewing projects by hand, creating a nearly invisible seam. It's also called a blind stitch. First, fold the two exposed edges under so you are looking at two folded edges. Knot the end of the thread, and insert from back to front of one folded edge, hiding the knot inside. Insert the needle from left to right, pick up a small piece of fabric from the top fold, and then a small piece of fabric directly under. Repeat from left to right. When you reach the end of the gap, knot the thread and bury the tails inside the project. No one will be the wiser!

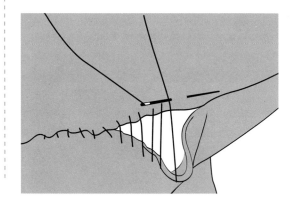

Apple pie in the oven, tell me you can taste lovin'.

Running stitch

Sewing doesn't get any simpler than this! Simply knot the end of your thread, and bring the needle from the back to the front of the fabric. Insert the needle down into the fabric and up again at regular intervals to create a dashed line of stitching. Use this stitch when you appliqué a felt shape in place.

Well, if you want these lumps, you gotta put a ring on it. WHERE'S MY RING?

Single crochet

Insert the crochet hook into the V shape of the crochet chain, as indicated in your pattern, or into the second chained stitch from the hook. Wrap the yarn around the hook and draw the yarn through the stitch.

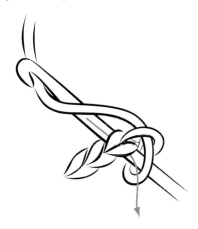

Now you have two loops on the hook. Wrap the yarn around the hook and draw the yarn through both stitches. You've just completed one single crochet.

Here are all the templates, charts, and patterns that were used to create the projects in this book. If a project instructs you to use a template to cut out fabrics, you have several options to transfer the templates in this book to the fabric.

Carbon transfer paper

You can buy this material in packs of multiple colors. One side of the paper is coated with a colored chalk that will rub off on fabric with pressure. Trace or photocopy the template onto a sheet of paper. Place the carbon paper on the fabric, and then place the tracing/photocopy on top of the carbon paper. Use a pen to trace over the design, pressing down hard so the coating on the carbon paper sticks to the fabric.

Tailor's chalk

If you don't have carbon paper, you can rub a piece of tailor's chalk all over one side of a sheet of plain paper. Then follow the instructions for carbon transfer paper to transfer the markings to the fabric.

Scissors

If you don't have any of the transfer materials just listed, simply photocopy or trace the templates printed in the book, then carefully cut out each piece with scissors or a craft knife. Pin the paper piece to the fabric (or simply hold it in place if it's small enough) and cut around the edges with fabric scissors.

ADVENTURE TIP
Never use your fabric scissors for anything other than fabric! Cutting paper dulls a blade very, very quickly.

FAN FICTION FINGER PUPPETS (page 10) | Copy at 200%

● French knot (page 126) — Back stitch (page 124)

Finn/Fionna's backpack

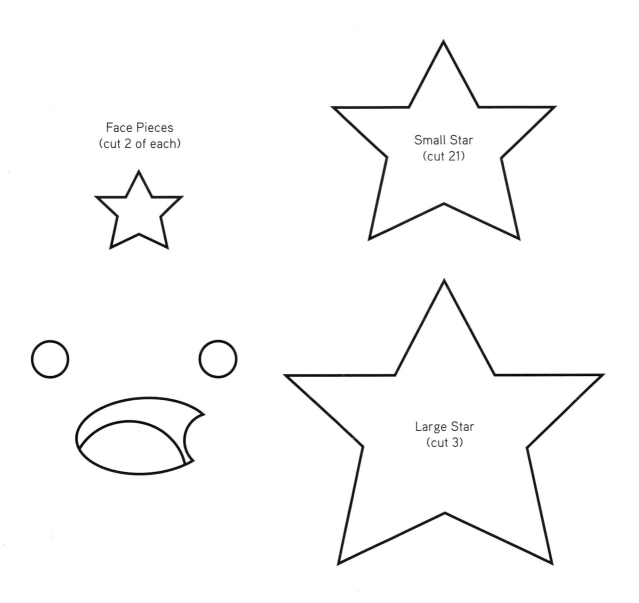

Face Pieces
(cut 2 of each)

Small Star
(cut 21)

Large Star
(cut 3)

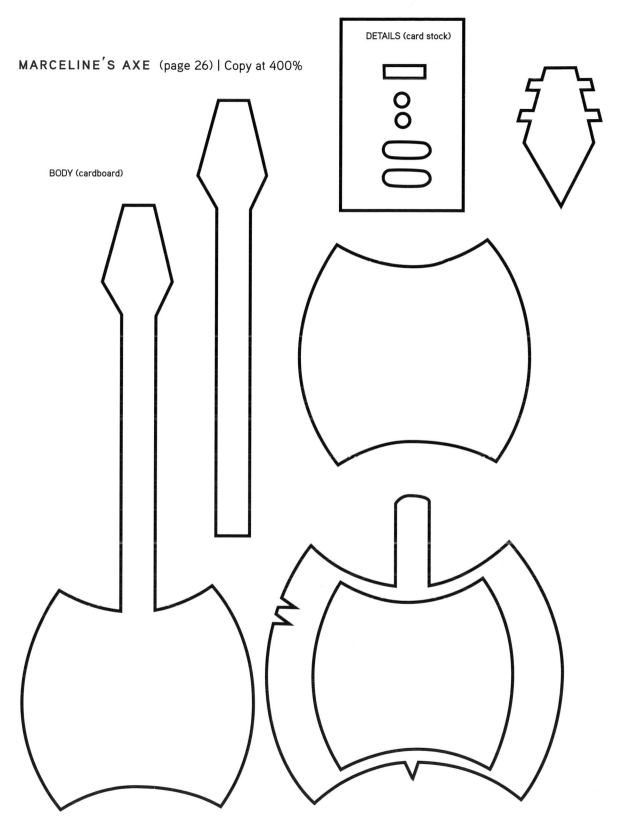

MARCELINE'S AXE (page 26) | Copy at 400%

BODY (cardboard)

DETAILS (card stock)

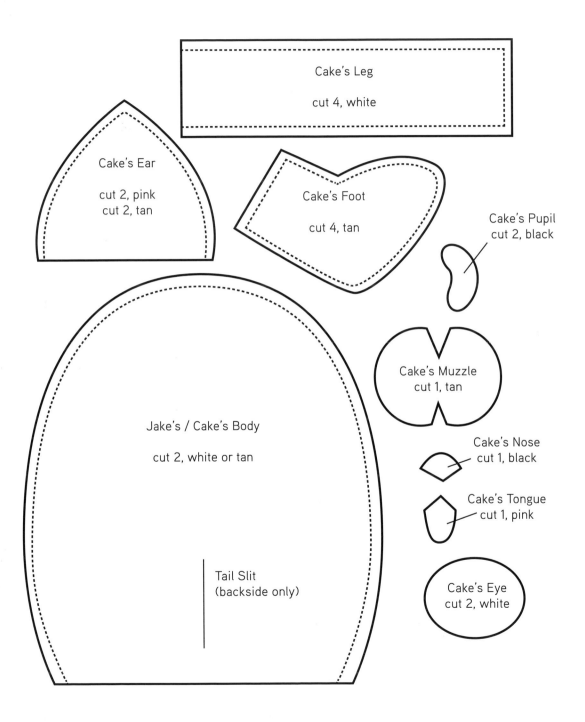

Cake's Leg

cut 4, white

Cake's Ear

cut 2, pink
cut 2, tan

Cake's Foot

cut 4, tan

Cake's Pupil
cut 2, black

Cake's Muzzle
cut 1, tan

Cake's Nose
cut 1, black

Cake's Tongue
cut 1, pink

Jake's / Cake's Body

cut 2, white or tan

Tail Slit
(backside only)

Cake's Eye
cut 2, white

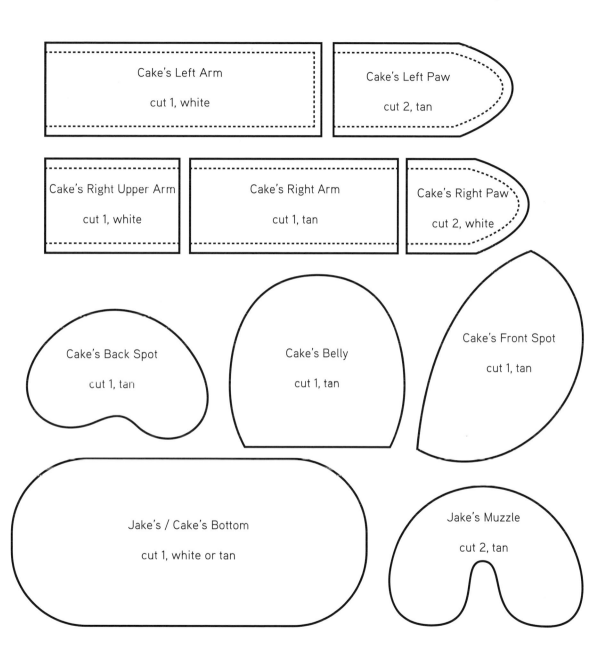

Cake's Left Arm

cut 1, white

Cake's Left Paw

cut 2, tan

Cake's Right Upper Arm

cut 1, white

Cake's Right Arm

cut 1, tan

Cake's Right Paw

cut 2, white

Cake's Back Spot

cut 1, tan

Cake's Belly

cut 1, tan

Cake's Front Spot

cut 1, tan

Jake's / Cake's Bottom

cut 1, white or tan

Jake's Muzzle

cut 2, tan

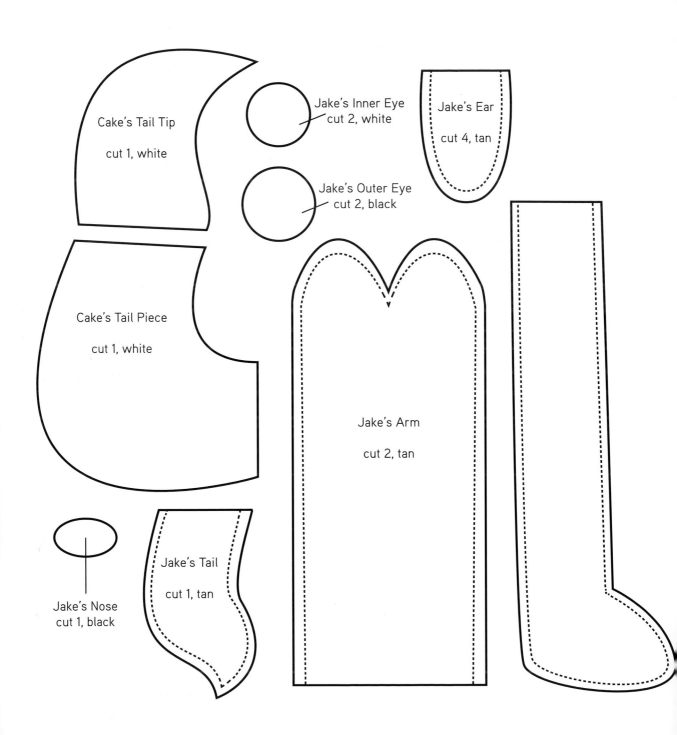

Cake's Tail Tip

cut 1, white

Jake's Inner Eye
cut 2, white

Jake's Ear

cut 4, tan

Jake's Outer Eye
cut 2, black

Cake's Tail Piece

cut 1, white

Jake's Arm

cut 2, tan

Jake's Nose
cut 1, black

Jake's Tail

cut 1, tan

PRINCESS HAIR ADORNMENTS (page 60) | Copy at 100%

- • French knot (page 126)
- — Back stitch (page 124)

WILDBERRY PRINCESS FASCINATOR (page 66) | Copy at 100%

- • French knot (page 126)
- — Back stitch (page 124)

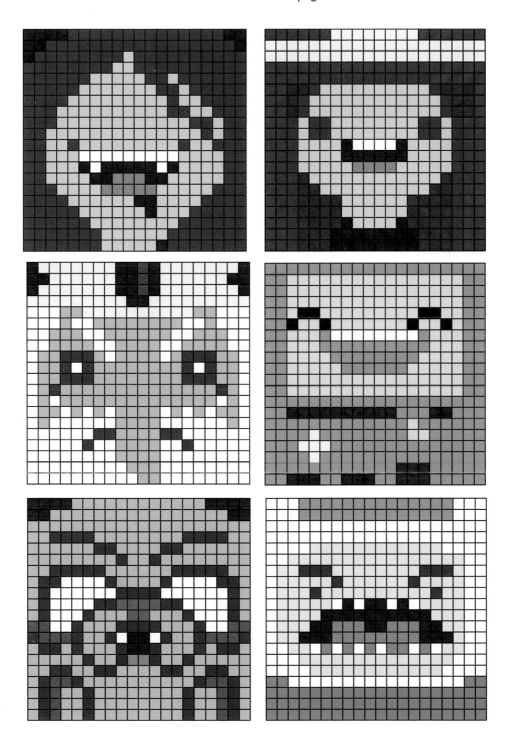

PEPPERMINT BUTLER PILLOW (page 79) | Copy at 200%

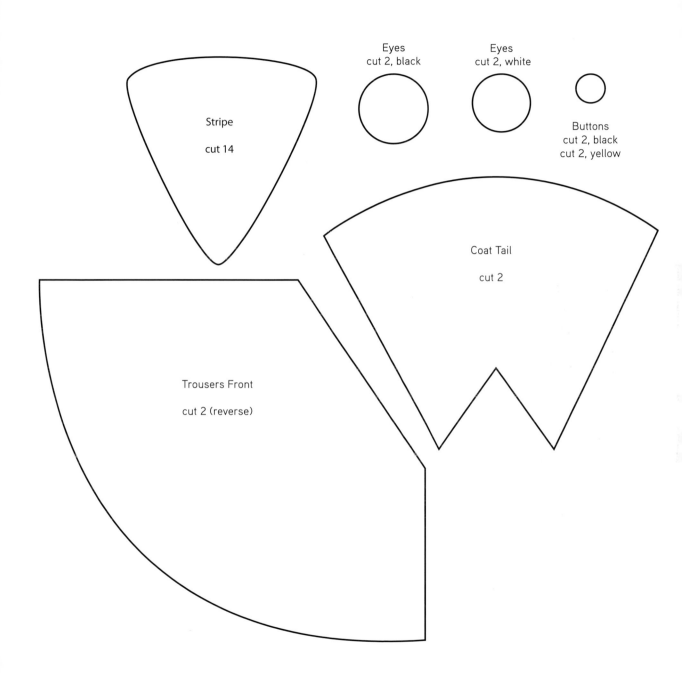

Stripe

cut 14

Eyes
cut 2, black

Eyes
cut 2, white

Buttons
cut 2, black
cut 2, yellow

Coat Tail

cut 2

Trousers Front

cut 2 (reverse)

FIONNA AND FINN HATS (page 94) | Copy at 250%

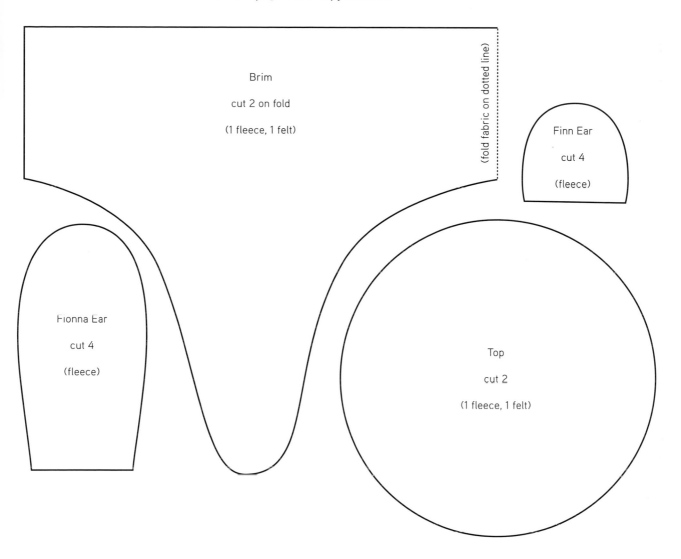

Brim

cut 2 on fold

(1 fleece, 1 felt)

(fold fabric on dotted line)

Finn Ear

cut 4

(fleece)

Fionna Ear

cut 4

(fleece)

Top

cut 2

(1 fleece, 1 felt)

BMO PHONE AND TABLET CASES (page 110) | Copy at 400% for a tablet case or 100% for a phone case

BUBBLEGUM'S LIKE-LIKE SWEATER (page 118)